SUNDAY
by
SUNDAY

KEN TAYLOR

SUNDAY
by
SUNDAY

MEDITATIONS AND RESOURCES FOR
ALL APPOINTED GOSPEL READINGS
YEARS A, B AND C
REVISED COMMON LECTIONARY

VOLUME ONE
ADVENT TO TRINITY

First published in 1999 by
KEVIN MAYHEW LTD
Buxhall
Stowmarket
Suffolk IP14 3BW

1 2 3 4 5 6 7 8 9

ISBN 1 84003 315 0
Catalogue No 1500243

Cover design by Jaquetta Sergeant
Edited by Peter Dainty
Typesetting by Louise Selfe
Printed and bound in Great Britain

Dedicated to my wife, Mary, especially
and to
Chris and Mark,
Andrew and Daniel
and Linsey

with thanks for all their help and encouragement

ABOUT THE AUTHOR

Ken Taylor is a Methodist minister. Born in Hull and trained in Manchester, he has worked in Orrell, St Helens, Liverpool (Crosby), Leeds (Cross Gates) and Chester-le-Street. He is married, with four sons and a daughter. Retired early through ill-health, he now lives in Skipton, where he still conducts worship and preaches most Sundays. He is the author of *Praying the Passion*, meditations and prayers for Lent (Kevin Mayhew 1996), and *Cradle of Hope*, meditations for Advent and Christmas (Kevin Mayhew 1997).

CONTENTS

FOREWORD

These meditations are intended both for devotional use and for resource purposes.

They are directly related to the Revised Common Lectionary, which is now being used by the large majority of English-speaking churches and by individual Christians. I find it exciting to know that, Sunday by Sunday, we are all hearing and exploring the same Scriptures.

Christian worship, by definition, celebrates and centres on the Gospel and so these meditations focus on the appointed Gospel reading for all three years.

Quite often, to accommodate the seasons between Advent and Trinity, the same Gospel is appointed for every year; and so these meditations are grouped by Sundays – with additional pieces for the few denominational variations. In the companion volume, from Trinity to Advent, meditations will be grouped by year.

As a resource book, I hope these meditations will prove a stimulus in sermon preparation and that the other occasional resources* which are included in this book will be of use in public worship.

The meditations may also prove a useful commentary for Bible study groups or a starting point for discussion in house-groups.

Privately, they may be used towards the end of a week in preparation for worship on the coming Sunday, or early in the week for recollection and action following the previous Sunday's worship.

It is always better to read the relevant gospel passage with the meditation.

KEN TAYLOR

* Italicised in Contents.

THE NAMING OF SUNDAYS _____

There are a few variations in the lectionaries which different denominations have appointed to accommodate their own needs. On most Sundays all English-speaking Christians will hear the same scriptures.

There is more variation, however, in the names given to some Sundays by different Churches. This book uses primarily the names used in the Church of England but the variations are listed below to avoid confusion for other Churches.

RCL	CHURCH OF ENGLAND	METHODIST	ROMAN CATHOLIC	URC; SCOTLAND
Baptism of the Lord	Baptism of Christ	Ordinary 1	Baptism of the Lord	Epiphany 1
Epiphany 2	Epiphany 2	Ordinary 2	Ordinary 2	Epiphany 2
Epiphany 3	Epiphany 3	Ordinary 3	Ordinary 3	Epiphany 3
Epiphany 4	Epiphany 4	Ordinary 4	Ordinary 4	Epiphany 4
Epiphany 5	Proper 1	Ordinary 5	Ordinary 5	Epiphany 5
Epiphany 6 *Proper 1*	Proper 2	Ordinary 6	Ordinary 6	Epiphany 6
Epiphany 7 *Proper 2*	Proper 3	Ordinary 7	Ordinary 7	Epiphany 7
Epiphany 8 *Proper 3*	Second before Lent	Ordinary 8	Ordinary 8	Epiphany 8
Epiphany Last	Transfiguration Sunday	Transfiguration Sunday	Ordinary 9	Transfiguration Sunday
Lent 5	Passion Sunday	Lent 5	Lent 5	Lent 5
Palm/Passion Sunday	Palm Sunday	Palm Sunday	Palm/Passion Sunday	Palm Sunday

ADVENT ———————————

Lord, come to us:
    in the loveliness of your compassion
    come.

Come with burning
    if you must;

    come with healing
    if you will;

    with peace,
    and joy,
    and love,
    come, Lord Jesus.

Further meditations for every day of the Advent and Christmas seasons can be found in Cradle of Hope *by the same author and publisher.*

First Sunday of Advent   **Year A:** *Matthew 24:36-44*
                              Year B: *Mark 13:24-37*
                              Year C: *Luke 21:25-36*

KEEP WATCHING _____

She buried her face in her hands
   in a corner made by school walls,
   and began to count;

   steadily at first,
   and then more quickly,
   and impatiently raced through the nineties,
   till she reached 100
   and the warning cry:
   'Coming, ready or not!'

So warn the Advent Gospels.

One day the world will end
   but none knows how or when;
   speculation is pointless.

But he who came in Galilee,
   and who will at the End bring all things into one
   is coming now:
   that's the challenge of Advent.

A figure crouches by a wall,
   'homeless and hungry' his cardboard reads:
   it looks like a ragged young man:
   but it's *him*.

Large bewildered eyes
    stare at you from the screen;
    it looks like a starving child:
    but it's *him.*

She wanders aimlessly down the street
    muttering to herself;
    another distressing case of Alzheimer's disease, you think:
    but it's *him.*

Day after day it's him –
    in an AIDS ward,
    in a dole queue,
    at a rehabilitation clinic,
    on a Childline,
    – wherever you look.

Nor is it only in cries for help that he comes
    but in joy and generosity,
    in kindness and caring,
    in courage and compassion,
    in forgiveness and reconciliation,
    in Creation and recreation.

Again and again, he comes to you
    in the ordinary things of life
    whether you are ready or not.

Advent is for waiting,
    waiting on the Lord
    in silence and stillness;

Advent is for watching
    to see what Christ is doing in the world

    and watching for Christ
    for when he comes to you;

Advent is for preparing,
    preparing ourselves
    so we are ready

    to recognise and respond to him
    when he comes.

Second Sunday of Advent   **Year A:** *Matthew 3:1-12*
Year B: *Mark 1:1-8*
Year C: *Luke 3:1-6*

The first Christians began the story of Jesus, not at Bethlehem,
but with an account of the ministry of John the Baptist.

THE PREPARATION _____

There had been no prophetic word
from the Lord of hosts for so long;

none like the great prophets of the Exile
for more than six hundred years.

Had the King of all the earth forsaken them?
Had the Holy One of Israel forgotten his chosen people?

They longed and looked for Elijah to come again
to announce the coming Messiah,
as Malachi had promised.

One day, travellers brought news to the city
of a preacher in the wilderness by Jordan,
dressed exactly as Scripture said Elijah was,
living on a simple, austere diet,
disdaining city comforts;

authentic and commanding in his presence,
rigorous and ruthless in his message.

Could this be the Prophet
    whom they looked for every Passover?

None knew where he'd come from;
    but suddenly he was there.

(Could he have been preparing
    with the community at Qumran?
So much of his teaching echoes theirs.)

He became the talk of the town;
    more and more travelled out to see him;

    Sadducees invited him to preach in Jerusalem
    but he would not leave the wilderness:

    if they wanted to hear him
    they must come to him –
    and they came – walking in the heat for hours!

He made 'crossing the Jordan' to come to him
    a symbolic frontier between old and new,
    like crossing the river with Joshua.

John did not invent baptism;
    Pharisees had devised it long before
    for Gentiles drawn to Jewish faith;
    with ritual circumcision and sacrifice,
    baptism would wash away the pollution of their former life.

John demanded a similar baptism of the Jews themselves
    for they too needed a rigorous new beginning.

Parentage, piety and prestige counted for nothing;
    stringent repentance and self-renunciation were essential.

Unbending and unshakeable,
  he demanded justice, honesty, and integrity,
  with warnings of impending doom
  as fierce as any of Amos or Elijah.

John faithfully prepared the ground,
  himself showed the humility he demanded:
  and gave the first priority to Jesus.

Repentance and humility are essential
  to receive and recognise Christ.

Third Sunday of Advent
Year A: *Matthew 11:2-11*
Year B: *John 1:6-8, 19-28*
Year C: *Luke 3:7-18*

After his wrestling in the wilderness, Jesus worked alongside John until the Baptist was arrested. If and how often and where they might have met together, if there was any pre-planning or deliberate collusion, can only be matters for speculation.

THE NEW DISPENSATION _____

John could not believe his ears!

He expected Messiah to develop his work
    but this dramatic change of emphasis
    was not what he expected.

There was no 'axe at the root of the trees',
    no 'separating wheat from chaff',
    no blazing judgement,
    no hell-fire holocaust,
    but healing, and acceptance, and sinners welcome.

There must be some mistake!

They were as different as chalk and cheese!

John threatened judgement,
    Jesus offered mercy.

John insisted they came to Jordan,
    Jesus went seeking the lost.

John was rigid, austere, unbending, puritanical,
    Jesus warm, compassionate, gentle and humble-hearted.

John demanded they improved by their own efforts;
    Jesus, the great encourager, offered help –
    'Come on, we'll make a new beginning together!'

The message was the same:
    Jesus still called for repentance,
    but took a further step
    into the dispensation of grace;

    from BC into AD,
    the realm of mercy and forgiveness,
    of help, and love, and liberty.

If John was 'the greatest man who ever lived'
    it seems harsh to put him outside the Kingdom;

    but he was 'outside',
    not because he was too early in time,
    but because his attitudes were wrong.

It's the difference between BC and AD.

Sometimes churches take John's hard line:
    we need to bring our BC attitudes and prejudice,
    into the light of Jesus and his love.

Jesus was not eight foot tall,
    nor had a light crown around his head;
    you could easily miss him in a crowd
    as you may have done today!

But John the Baptist knew him
   and could point him out to others.

The better we know Jesus,
   talk with him and grow with him,
   the more easily we shall recognise him
   when he comes.

MARY'S SECRET

She had a share in the catering
    for a village wedding at Cana-in-Galilee.

When the wine ran out
    she went to the servants' area
    and proudly pointed them to Jesus:
    'That's my son over there;
    I'll ask him to come and help.

'When he comes
    do whatever he says.

'Even if you don't understand,
    even if it sounds crazy,
    do whatever he says:
    you can trust him.'

This was the sure ground
    of her own obedience.

Such pure, profound and simple faith
    came most naturally to her.
She could not remember a time
    when she had questioned it.

It had sustained her
> in most difficult and demanding days . . .

When afraid of Gabriel's greeting
> and of what was being asked of her:
> 'I am the Lord's servant.
I will do whatever he says, and I will trust him.'

When Joseph was suspicious
> and neighbours' comments hurt her,
> 'We must do whatever he says: and trust him.'

As her baby grew
> this was the fundamental faith she taught him.

Though like all the other children,
> she saw a growing 'otherness' in him
> and felt him growing away from her;
> she sensed more of the Eternal in his eyes and words,
> and dreaded the day he must leave home;

> even in the 'sunshine' years
> she often recalled old Simeon's warning,
> and wondered what coming years would bring;

> but whatever her commitment to her Lord might cost,
> she would do whatever he said – and trust him.

Her sure and steadfast faith, so plain at Cana,
> is one with the strongest and best in Israel's story:

> Noah building a boat on dry land under blue skies,
> Abraham not sure of his destination but travelling on,
> Moses standing before Pharaoh,
> young David going to meet Goliath,

Elijah on Carmel, defeating the prophets of Baal,
Amos leaving his flocks in response to God's call,
Jeremiah buying a plot of land in a desolate country,
Isaiah in exile, certain of deliverance.

Even if you don't understand,
  even if it seems crazy,
  even if it hurts,

  do whatever he says,
  and trust him.

CHRISTMAS _____

CHRIST IS COME

with Peace that passes all understanding,

with Joy that no one shall take from us,

with Love stronger than anything
else in the whole creation.

Serve and celebrate him.

Christmas Eve and Christmas Day   **All years:** *Luke 2:1-14*
                                               Luke 2:8-20
                                               John 1:1-14

CHRIST COMES

Every sign and symbol of that first Christmas
 is worth turning in your mind
 to find the truth it holds:

  journeys and a crowded pub,
  family reunions and presents,
  travellers and workers,
  lonely old people,
  suffering children. . . .

Christmas is about normal days
 and familiar situations that seem far removed
 from the tinsel-trimmed time-out we have devised . . .

  and at the centre of it all, a Child;
  born in the night,
  he brings light to our darkness.

God comes in unexpected ways,
 with no stamping of feet or trumpet-blast,
 and no little label to say who the gift is from.

The manner and the means,
 the people and the place,
 would never make you think of *God*.

Christmas is full of surprises
   and this surprising God
   has more surprises still in store for us.

The year turns in the midst of Christmas days;
   as always our changing times
   are set within the eternal Purpose;

   with the echoes of angelic assurance
   that there is no need to be afraid:

This is the perfect Love
   that casts out fear.

The story does not end
   when shepherds go home
   and the world achieves its annual ritual of forgetting.

Suddenly, we're back in the familiar world
   of political tyrants, and refugee families,
   and the senseless slaughter of children.

It is in this world,
   with its harsh and bitter realities,
   that Christ comes to us,

   not waiting for us to come to him,
   not only beyond us
   but beside us.

In that well-known Christmas song
    an over-zealous lover bestows on his beloved
    184 birds, 168 visitors, 40 cows, and 40 golden rings!

The song is right:
    Love is consistent and reliable and generous.

What he gives is new every morning,
    and the blessings and benefits increase as time goes by.

THE CHRIST WHO COMES

> We celebrate the birth of this Child
> because of the man he grew to be

While we build a Nativity crib in one transept, we could also build a still-life montage of symbols of the life and ministry of Jesus in the other.

At a suitable point during the annual Carol service, young people or children carrying these symbols process singly through the congregation.

They move, in turn, into the centre of the chancel, present their symbol to the congregation, reciting the words below, and then proceed to the transept where the montage display is gradually assembled.

Only as the first person moves from the centre is the second symbol processed in; and so on.

leader
We celebrate the birth of this Child
only because of the man he grew to be.

We recall this night
not only the story of his birth
but build a montage of symbols of the man,
of what he said and did.

child with
loaf of
bread
Jesus said:
I am the Bread of life.
Whoever comes to me shall never be hungry.

child with
shepherd's
crook
Jesus said:
I am the Good Shepherd,
and I lay down my life for the sheep.

child with
chalice

Jesus said:
I am the true Vine.
Anyone who dwells in me
as I dwell in him
bears much fruit.

two children
with **towel**
and basin

Jesus said:
The son of man
came not to be served
but to serve.

child with
cross

Jesus said:
I am Resurrection
and I am Life.
He who believes in me shall never die.

child with
manger

Jesus said:
I am come that they might have life,
life in all its fullness.

leader

Christmas means
that God is with you now,
sharing every situation.

FULFILLING PROPHECIES _____

Matthew needed to convince his readers
    that his book was worth reading.

They were looking for Messiah
    so 'proof' texts were very important.

Matthew set out his claim:

    Prophets foretold Messiah will be . . .

        descended from Abraham: Jesus was
        born of a virgin: Jesus was
        born in Bethlehem: Jesus was,

    and so onwards in his Gospel . . .

        worshipped by kings from afar,
        accompanied by weeping, as Jeremiah said,
        coming from Egypt,
        called a Nazarene.

This must be proof enough.

This Jesus is Messiah,
    King of Israel, Lion of Judah.

He is all that the prophets foretold:
    he is the promised One:
    now read on . . .

    Matthew made the story fit the texts,
    bent the tale if need be;

and there had to be seven texts,
a perfect seven, of course.

Proof texts and Scripture quotes
were so important in the early Church
to show fulfilling of the promises
and continuity of the faith.

Prophets seldom 'foretold' the future,
except predictions of consequence:
'If you do that, this will surely happen; but if not . . .',

normally prophets 'told forth'
the truth that they could see
of what the Lord was doing in their time.

That's the point –
that God was working in their time
as he is always working in his world.

He has been here all the time,
so involved in his creation,
so committed to his creatures,
that Incarnation was the logical consequence
of his redeeming care.

The revelation in Jesus
was no sudden swoop from heaven,
no single intervention in human affairs
coming like the cavalry in the nick of time to save us.

The continuity matters very much.

It is still the way it has always been:
God is still working in his world.

If you look, you will see what he is doing;
if you will, you can work with him.

Luke's story of the Presentation in the Temple is repeated on Epiphany 4 (C) and for the feast day on February 2nd.

THE HIDDEN YEARS ─────────────

Pious religious overtones miss the point.
Jesus was simply growing up like anybody else.

There were many fanciful stories about his childhood,
    like those about a bird, a fish, a dog,
    and his first girl-friend!

But it's most important we know nothing:
    the 'hiddenness' is very precious;
    nothing startling happened,
    and he grew just as you did.

Incarnation means that he was truly human:
    had to learn to walk, to talk,
    to dress, to feed himself.

Incarnation was no static package,
    not a solid lump of holy revelation,
    but a living, breathing, growing lad,
    learning as he grew.

He watched Mary making bread,
    watched Joseph at the bench,
    and learned to be a carpenter.

He played with other children,
    played weddings and funerals often;
    walked along the riverside,
    roamed the hills alone.

One day, when he was eight,
    he woke to see a plume of black smoke,
    hanging in the eastern sky.

As the day wore on
    they learned how Roman soldiers had set fire to Sepphoris,
    burned the whole town and many of its people –
        as a reprisal;
    Jesus grew up in a violent, occupied country.

The one authenticated story
    is of his Barmitzvah journey to Jerusalem.

My earliest impression of this tale
    was how the wisest scholars crowded round
    to ask for information from this holy child from heaven!

But it was *he* who was asking the questions!

More spiritually sensitive than others,
    excited by his first glimpse of the Temple,
    he seized the chance to ask the greatest scholars
    about the prophets and the Law and their traditions;
    and lost all track of time.

Like any other teenager,
    he asserted his independence;
    he was growing up – and away from his parents.

And his parents had to let him go;
    we must all hold our children precious,
    safe and sure, but with open hands
    – as we hold Communion bread.

The lad was growing up,
    in body, mind and spirit,
    with a growing awareness and otherness,
    till he received the Spirit
    and fully became what he was meant to be.

The prologue of the Fourth Gospel is the greatest piece of Christian writing. John introduces all the great themes of Life and Light, Judgement and Truth, Grace and Glory, that he will weave like golden threads throughout his book. He uses ideas familiar to both his Greek and Jewish readers. He makes the most profound and penetrating statement of Christian faith.

THE MYSTERY OF THE INCARNATION

'The Word became flesh'
    is the climax of John's prologue
    and the bed-rock of Christian faith.

The eternal God,
    the unknowable, invisible Ground of being,
    who is beyond anything we can imagine,
    is made plain to us,
    in flesh and blood terms
    that we can understand,
    in Jesus of Nazareth.

Both Jews and Greeks were familiar
    with the concept of the logos,
    more than simply the spoken word,
    but the powerful agent of creation,
    the dynamic eternal purpose of God.

And then John took the most startling step,
    the entirely new, incredible step,
    unthinkable to any Jewish scholar,

beyond any Greek speculation,
and claimed that the eternal Word became a man.

Not simply a phantom,
    nor a mere appearance or pretence,
    but really took our human nature
    and was truly and fully a man.

He dwelt among us,
    pitched his tent with us,
    'tabernacled' with us,
    (the word needs savouring),
    and we can actually see with our own eyes
    the Shekinah-glory of the Lord,
    and the prophetic dream is a reality:
    God in the midst of his people.

God makes himself in our image;
    Jesus is entirely one with God,
    in heart and mind and being;
    he is the human face of God.

If we have seen Jesus
    we have seen what God is like.

Jesus is as much of God as anyone can grasp.

At the end of a long childhood's day
    spent happily on a beach,
    someone brought a bucketful of sea-water
    to wash the sand from our feet.

When it was my turn to fetch the water,
    I filled the bucket to the brim,
    and walked so carefully back,

not to spill a drop.
It was as much of the sea as I could carry.

One could learn so much about the sea
    from that one bucketful:

    its taste,
    its specific gravity and density,
    its atomic and molecular structure,
    its very essence;

    but not its unfathomable depths,
    its diverse currents or majestic power,
    from that one bucketful.

Jesus is like a 'bucketful' of God.

Limited to one time and place,
    not knowing everything,
    and not omnipotent,
    he is not identical with God.

But he brings the very essence of God
    within our grasp;
    he is as much of God as human minds can carry.

The more clearly we see Jesus
    the more we shall know the very heart of God.

But Jesus also shows us
    the heart of true humanity,
    the vision of what we may become.

If we can be 'brimful' of him,
    in mind and heart,
    we shall become what we were meant to be;
    made in the image of God.

NO DISTANCE AT ALL

A well-known and popular song is entitled 'From a distance'.

It has a very pleasant tune and I fully appreciate the sentiment expressed in the lyrics, but in the light of the Incarnation the theology is very wide of the mark.

I have suggested the following to some vocalists as an additional final verse to Christianise the song:

He is one with us,
    he's alongside us,
    he has come to us
        from a distance.

He is healing hurt,
    he's forgiving wrong,
    he is close to us,
        not at a distance.

He's the Hope of hopes,
    he's the Love of loves
    in the heart of every man.

He is saving us,
    he's uniting us,
    he has come to us
        from a distance.

He is close to us –
Not at a distance.

EPIPHANY _____

Lighten our darkness,
   we beseech you, O Lord,
   the darkness around us,
   the darkness within us,
   this darkness of the heart and mind
   which we have designed for ourselves.

Lighten our darkness,
   we beseech you, O Lord,
   the shadowy parts of our lives,
   the twilight world where we are content to live,
   the darkness of the shadow of death.

Lighten our darkness,
   we beseech you, O Lord,
   and by your great mercy
   deliver us from all the perils and dangers
   of this night which we have made.

Deliver us from being in the dark
   for the sake of your only Son,
   our Saviour Jesus Christ.

                             Amen.

LIGHT FOR THE WORLD _____

They were not kings but astrologers:
    God speaks to secular men
    who seek their future in the stars.

They were not Jews but foreigners
    who did not know the prophets;
    but God has no favourites.

Love has no prejudice
    of race, religion, class or gender:
    Christ is for everyone.

Their gifts were hardly appropriate.

Jesus was not interested in gold:
    what you *are* is more important than what you have;

    his religion was as wide as life
    and not confined to special rituals;

    and when Mary came with myrrh
    to embalm his corpse,
    he was up and gone.

Their gifts are *symbols* of Christ,
    King of kings,
    High Priest in the order of Melchizedek
    and Saviour of the world by his dying.

But, even more,
>   their gifts are symbols of their world,
>   where money was power,
>   and religion a superstitious burden,
>   where there was much suffering,
>   and everything grew old and died.

In effect, they offered themselves and their world to him.

His birth marked a new beginning
>   which also meant they had come to an end.

Their world was ending
>   with the dawn of a new one;
>   the old order was finished;
>   a new day had come.

Their journey was a long pilgrim-search for truth,
>   and, as so often, much of it in darkness,
>   with only the glimmer of his light,
>   beckoning onwards.

God started where they were
>   and led them by an unexpected path
>   to an unexpected place,
>   and at their journey's end a most surprising King.

It takes patience and persistence
>   to follow the light of love
>   and search out truth.

Travel by whatever light you have,
>   and be prepared to find him
>   in unexpected places and unexpected people.

Christ, who guides us all the way,
>   is at our journey's end.

The Baptism of Christ
Ordinary 1

Year A: *Matthew 3:13-17*
Year B: *Mark 1:4-11*
Year C: *Luke 3:15-17, 21f*

This was the most formative day in Jesus' life. From his intense religious experience in the river Jordan came the unshakeable, burning conviction that dominated his life.

THE MOST IMPORTANT DAY _____

Unaware of burdening sins,
 Jesus came to be baptised by John.

People were responding to John's preaching
 and he wanted to be with them,
 alongside them,
 fully immersed in being human.

God was clearly working in John's ministry
 so Jesus identified himself with it,
 and by his sharing and submission
 was himself open to God's presence.

He came out of the river,
 water streaming down his face and hair,
 muffling the voices on the riverbank.

But one clear strong and steady Voice
 filled his head and heart:
 You are my Son. . . .

This was breathtaking. . . .

For years he'd had a growing awareness
    of a special work he had to do
    but this exceeded anything he'd dreamed of.

Many had called God 'Father' before
    but never like this –
    not with such intensity
    or the intimacy of *Abba*.

All his life was grounded here:
    his message, and mission, and purpose,
    all his attitudes, and actions, and teaching.

God is Abba, your Father,
    and, like a little child, you can trust him.

Whatever your condition or your present need
    he understands and shares,
    and is alongside you.

You never know
    when this surprising God will come to you:
    so don't be missing when the table is set,
    or when his people meet,
    for that could be the day.

And don't be surprised
    that he speaks to you
    or by what he says.

God is Abba,
    and you can trust him
    far more than you do.

Lord, I too have been baptised,
    signed with your sign, marked out for you;
    help me to learn and grow in faith and love.

Second Sunday after Epiphany   **Year A:** *John 1:29-42*
Ordinary 2   **Year B:** *John 1:43-51*

John begins one of his major themes – the testimony of
witnesses to the identity of Jesus.

The Word-made-flesh is recognised as Lamb of God,
Rabbi, Messiah, fulfiller of the prophecies, Son of God and
King of Israel, and far greater than Jacob – he is himself the
ladder joining earth and heaven.

COME AND SEE

When they meet Christ
   each finds what they really need:

      Andrew finds more than he expected;
      searching Philip finds the man to follow;

      Simon is given a new name,
      new potential and new purpose;
      Nathanael finds a challenge to his prejudice
      and an answer to his prayers.

The insistent 'Come and see'
   invites them to new understanding,

      a new understanding of Jesus,
      and of themselves.

There is more to Jesus than they expected,
   and he has more important things to show them
   about God and how he works,
   about the Kingdom and what it means,
   about the way of love.

It doesn't come in a moment;
  there is no blinding revelation;

  but 'come' and 'see' belong together:
  as they travel with him
  he will lead them to more of the truth.

He has surprising and exciting things to show them
  about light and life, about true glory,
  and about the way of love
  which they will find is the way of the cross,
  and the only way to life eternal. . . .

Andrew brings Simon,
  Philip brings Nathanael;
  most new disciples still
  are brought by one they know and trust.

Still he insists we 'come and see'.

We each shall find in him
  what we really need.

And he has so much to teach us,
  unexpected and exciting things:
  about himself
  and God and his ways,
  and the truth about glory and power,
  and about his Kingdom of love.

Seeing is believing
  but believing is not faith:
  for faith is trust.

Still he invites to come and see
  until we understand enough
  and trust him enough
  to become what we are meant to be.

QUITE A PARTY _____

He loved parties and company
    and delighted in this simple village wedding,
    always glad to share in others' happiness.

He was himself great fun to be with;
    not yet a man of sorrows, he was a man of joy –
    and there was so much laughter in the early days.

Cana was not far from Nazareth,
    and Mary may have shared the preparations,
    her concern reflecting some responsibility.

In need she turns to him
    (as she has for some years now);
    and his gentle rebuke
    reveals the strong love between them.

And she submits to him
    and trusts him:
    'Do whatever he tells you'.

With 180 gallons of wine,
    far more than they needed,
    it must have been some party!

That's the clearest clue
    that there's more to this story than meets the eye
    – a deeper level.

In John's wonderful book
     there are always deeper meanings:

'On the third day' is a hint:
look for links with the resurrection
and the new life Jesus brings.

It's a wedding –
     a new beginning in a new relationship,

and points to 'the heavenly banquet
which he has prepared for all',
the great marriage feast of the Lamb,
with Christ the Bridegroom and the Church his Bride,
at one with him and under his authority.

Six is less than seven – and so imperfect –

and to make sure you get the point,
six jars are identified with Jewish Law
and symbolise a religion that's imperfect,
even for those brimful of it.

It is superseded by the new,
     now the Perfecter has come.

Water is transformed by his presence,
     as is all life:
a better religion and a better life,
a new and richer quality of life,
as different as water and wine.

The sign of glory linking human and divine
     is the transformation Jesus brings,
     and the humility that shares with ordinary folk.

He saves best till last –
     the further you follow him the better it gets;
     and as the years pass by
     this is the hope I treasure:
     he saves the best till last.

COME WITH ME

They'd talked with him and heard him speaking,
    had never met anyone so inspiring,
      wondered if he could be the promised One.

That morning
    they saw him coming while he was some way off;
    and pretended to be busy with their nets,
    heads bent, but watching through their eyebrows . . .

    as he drew level with them,
    they looked up with feigned surprise
    and caught his eye and smiled a hesitant greeting;

    and he stopped,
    and spoke to *them*,
    and their hearts pounded.

Just to be with him
    would be beyond their wildest dreams;

    and to be of use to him,
    give new direction to their gifts and skills
    – their response was eager and immediate.

Jesus felt that time was short
    and the urgency required he had some help.

From his many disciples,
>   he would choose some
>   whom he could train and send on mission:
>   apostles of the Kingdom.

Deliberately he would choose twelve –
>   twelve would be a sign of his New Israel;
>   sent out in two's,
>   they would increase the preaching sevenfold.

He began steadily collecting those whom he wanted.

They were a mixed bunch:
>   five were fishers, one a business-man, four had been zealots,
>   three pairs of brothers, several were already friends,
>   only one southerner.

They had complementing or conflicting temperaments –
>   impetuous, cautious, arrogant, humble,
>   perceptive, hesitant, quick-tempered,
>   one sure that he was right –

>   and they had to learn to live and work together.

But most of all
>   they had to learn from him,
>   they had so much to learn from him
>   about God, and the Kingdom,
>   the world, and other people, and themselves,
>   and about love.

Still he comes
>   and calls you by your name,
>   calls for your skills and gifts
>   for the service of the Kingdom.

We give ourselves to him
   – and he gives us to each other:
   and we have to learn to live and work together
   with all who follow him.

And we have so much to learn from him.

HOMECOMING ————————————————

The crown-prince of the prophets,
   whose name we do not know,
   saw more clearly than any other
   the truth at the heart of God;
   his poems were added to what Isaiah had written[*]
   two hundred years before.

His songs were favourites of Jesus
   since first hearing them in childhood;
   they so inspired him that he lived them.

Whoever was the original subject of the poems,
   Jesus alone embodied in himself
   this faithful Servant of the Lord.

His work in Galilee was well established
   before he came to Nazareth.
Luke sets this story in the earliest days,
   like a manifesto of the ministry that follows.

When invited to preach in Nazareth,
   whether the reading was appointed for the day
   or of Jesus' own choosing,
   no Scripture better suited his proclamation.

[*] Isaiah 42:1-7; 49:1-6; 50:4-9; 52:13-53:12

They were excited in Nazareth
    that their Jesus was coming home.
(If he had come to stay,
    imagine what visiting crowds would do for trade!)

Sitting down to address them,
    he confirmed what they had heard:
    he was a very good preacher indeed.

Did they take too literally what he said
    about poverty and liberty and healing,
    while he intended deeper, spiritual meanings?

But pleasure and approval turned to criticism
    when they saw what he was claiming.

He was getting above himself;
    after all, they'd watched him grow,
    gone to school with him,
    and played with him;
    he was one of their own lads.

And criticism turned to violent anger
    when he implied God favoured Gentiles.
Who did he think he was,
    with his new ideas and arrogant claims?

They thought he was *their* Jesus,
    that he belonged to them,
    but he could not be constrained by their ideas
    nor his vision restricted by theirs.

We can never possess him
though he may possess us.

We can never use his friendship
to service our own ends.

However well we think we know him,
he has new truth to teach us,
new visions to share with us.

TRUE CONTENTMENT

When you know that you need help
    from beyond yourself and accept it,
    God will work in your life.

When you are moved to caring action
    by the suffering of other people,
    you will be given the strength to love.

When you channel all your resources
    into the way of love,
    you are of that company
    through whom the world is saved.

When you work continually
    for justice and peace,
    you will achieve both.

When you forgive
    even those who have hurt you very deeply,
    you will know the joy and liberty
    of being yourself forgiven, at one with God.

When love is working in your heart,
    you will see God in other people
    and understand how he is working.

When you make peace
    and work for reconciliation,
    you will become what you are meant to be.

All this is very costly,
you may well suffer for it;

but it is the privilege of sharing
in what God is doing in the world,
and of being his child.

IN CORPORATE WORSHIP

This paraphrase of the Beatitudes can be used effectively in a
dialogue of two voices for meditation in corporate worship.

The first reads one Beatitude from Matthew's text;
the other responds with the corresponding paraphrase;
with a following short silence for individual reflection.

IN THE SYNAGOGUE

Capernaum was the centre of his ministry in Galilee,
and on Saturday he went to synagogue.

Although Mark gives no record,
you can imagine what he said;
it was certainly not what they expected.

He announced the coming of the Kingdom,
spoke of God's mercy and forgiveness,
of help and hope and liberty,
and joy in believing.
It was like a breath of fresh air.

The *manner* of his teaching
was more astounding than the content.

If he caught your eye, it was arresting;
each one felt that he was talking just to them.

And he spoke with such authority,
not quoting other teachers,
nor underpinning his arguments with other sayings;

in fact he presented no argument
but a simple statement of fact.

It seemed like a message straight from God.
They had never heard anything like this before.

One man was especially affected.

Most of the time he was fine,
or he would have been excluded
from society and the synagogue.

Today the electric atmosphere and excited buzz around him
aroused his nervous tension and provoked this outburst.

You may not believe in demons and ascribe his symptoms
to hysteria or epilepsy or a disease we recognise.

But demon-belief was common in the ancient world,
as in this congregation and the man himself.

The wonder in this synagogue
was not only that the man was cured;
the manner of it was more surprising than the fact.

There was no incanted list of spirit-names
to find a stronger or higher spirit,
as was standard practice for the many exorcists;

Jesus simply commanded and it was done.

He seemed to have the necessary power
in his own strength and person.

Mark compiled this short symposium
of the authority of Jesus –
with fishermen,
and in his teaching, and with a man possessed.

There was never anyone like Jesus.

He speaks the truth about God;
he can meet your need;
and he can set you free.

also Feast of Presentation (2 February)

GROUND OF HOPE

Simeon was the kind of old man
    many men would like to grow to be
    – kind and gentle, benign and strong,
    with a twinkle in his eyes;
    and a great encourager of the young.

Delighting in his memories,
    accepting the limits of ageing,
    without discontent or resignation,

    accepting his failures in life
    as well as his achievements,
    he was at peace with himself,
    and the world,
    and God.

He had kept the faith,
    he had almost finished the course,
    his hope as firm and keen as ever,
    sure that God keeps his promises.

He came often to the Temple,
    glad of an old man's ample time to pray,
    certain God keeps his promises,
    and that he would see salvation;
    – would it be today?

Many, holding their first grandchild,
    gasp with wonder at Creation –
    and such perfect finger-nails –
    and find calm in the continuity
    and the mystery of generations.

But holding this Child was more than that:
    this One was special.

It was more than joy
    in the potential of a new generation
    – he saw hope for the world,
    as well as for himself
    in the light in the eyes of this Child.

He knew deep peace to be assured
    that, just as he held this Child in his hands,
    so God was holding *him* in his.

From his long experience of life and God
    he could advise and warn these parents,
    and perceive the prospect for the Child.

Like many other widows, Anna,
    in her bereavement, found firmer faith
    and strength in the community of believers,
    and in prayer with them and privately.

These two were among the 'Quiet in the Land',
    looking for the Kingdom through no violent victories
    or grasping power by force of arms,
    but content to wait in patient prayer and worship
    until he come.

To grow old gracefully
    it's better to start young;
    but at any age or stage of life
    be sure God holds you in his hands.

To 'depart in peace'
    depends on trusting him,
    believing that God keeps his promises
    and keeps the best till last.

WORTH ITS SALT ————————————————

Before we had freezers
    they salted ham to preserve it,
    and 'put down' eggs.

I cut my foot on the beach,
    and they sent me into the stinging sea
    because it cleans and heals, they said.

Despite its 'bad press' lately,
    cooks still use salt to 'bring out the taste'
    or things would be insipid.

A church that's worth its salt
    has truths to preserve
    but only what's worth keeping.

Moving to a smaller house,
    so many books and furniture wouldn't fit
    we had to decide what really matters
    and jettison the rest.

A church that's worth its salt
    does not cart junk around
    nor is it so cluttered that it cannot move.

A church that's worth its salt
    makes time and place for healing,
    rediscovers that neglected ministry,

and works for reconciliation, wholeness, healing,
within a church and between the churches,
in families and in community,
within this nation and in the world.

A church that's worth its salt
enriches people's lives;

so many want their life to be worth living,
chase happiness in the wrong directions,
and have false expectations
of themselves or others or life itself.

A church that's worth it's salt
has truth to preserve,
healing to channel,
and offers life and light.

A church that's worth its salt
knows where it stands,
and stands there –

knows where it stands,
not on trivia
but on really important issues,
the things people lie awake worrying about.

Being light to the world
means helping people to see more clearly.

And as the only light we have is his,
who is himself the light of the world;
we have to reflect him.

This Sunday's lection also introduces Jesus' attitude to the
Law which is the subject of other lections and meditations,
especially those on pages 70-72, 75-78 and 81-83.

ON THE DOORSTEP

Word of what happened in the synagogue
   spread quickly through the town;

    with three stars visible after sun-down
    and the Sabbath over,
    scribal law permitted carrying the sick.

When Simon opened the door
   it seemed that all Capernaum was there,
   aching and in desperate need.

It was what Jesus half-expected,
   but he had not sought it.

His primary task was preaching:

    the immanence of the Kingdom
    made the proclamation urgent;
    and he felt time so short
    he soon appointed twelve to do the work.

His healing work was secondary for him.
He did not go in search of sufferers;
   they came looking for him;
   help and relief from pain were uppermost for them.

He understood their need
   and when confronted by disease or need
   he quickly moved to help;
   in that moment the sufferers were his first priority.

He saw the wholeness he created as itself
    a sign of the presence of the Kingdom.

But it was all so demanding,
    not only because there was so much need,
    but meeting it took so much out of him

And the days were so full;
    if Mark's diary for a typical day*
    is anything to go by,
    they kept him very busy.

Deep sleep and solitary early prayer
    were essential for his recuperation.

As yet he did not know
    that there would come a sleepless night
    and a day when all the needs of all the people
    would take all he had to give.

For the people his authority was astounding,
    his stories entertaining,
    but his gift for healing met immediate need
    and they wanted healing even more than truth.

No wonder they were looking for him everywhere.

What need is waiting on your doorstep?

Should help for any of your neighbours
    have a higher priority for you?

And who is your neighbour?

* See Mark 1:21-39.

Luke's version of the call of the first disciples differs from the others and has clear links with John's post-resurrection story of Jesus and Simon at the lakeside (John 21).

CALLING SIMON

Simon was finishing his work
    after a long frustrating night,
    tired and longing for his bed,

    but was intrigued to lend his boat
    – it had never been used by a Rabbi before.
It was like a lakeside synagogue.

Such ingenuity caught his imagination,
    but not so much as what the man was saying.
He had such skill with words,
    painted such vivid pictures,
    and clearly knew what he was talking about.

Jesus, turning from the crowd,
    saw sunlight glint on fishes' fins . . .

    and Simon, captivated by the man and by his teaching,
    tired as he was, agreed to put to sea again
    'If you say so . . .'

    and then there were so many fishes;
    after such a barren night
    it seemed like a miracle.

This unlearned fisherman
    felt most unworthy,
    with such a passenger
    of such dignity, authority, and mastery;

    and what seemed like a miracle
    made him feel afraid.

'Don't be frightened:
    come with me'.

'If you say so. . . .'

Still Christ comes to us
    at our daily work;

    and especially when we are just tired,
    or feel we have achieved nothing,
    he comes.

He still has important things to say to us,

    and still can see what we can't:
    the answer to what we have been seeking.

Why do we get so frightened
    and try to keep him at arms' length?

We want the benefits of his presence
    but don't want to be disturbed.

Are we so afraid of what he will ask of us,
    where he will lead us,
    what he might do to us,
    that we put up shutters against him?

All he asks
    is that we take his word to heart,
    and do what he says,
    take his new direction,
    and trust him.

'If you say so, I will . . .'
    . . . and the miracle begins.

LAW AND GRACE

The Law,
    given by God through Moses,
    was their strength and their delight,
    their security against heresy,
    and reason for their long survival.

Jesus claimed to fulfil the Law –
    but not the pernickety applications,
    (like 617 rules to keep the Sabbath),
    argued endlessly by the scribes,
    observed meticulously by Pharisees,
    which he openly contradicted and ignored
    or deliberately broke.

He spoke with impressive authority;
    they'd never heard anything like it before.

He took the lid off the Law of God,
    went deeper than any had done before,
    struck to the very heart of the matter,
    which is a matter of the human heart.

It's not enough
    to avoid the outward actions Moses banned:
    what about your heart?

Attitude matters as much as action.

Killing is wrong,
    but so is nursing a grievance or a grudge.

Nursing anger is bad,
    but contempt and snobbery are worse,
    malicious gossip is worst of all.

When people have fallen out
    does it really matter whose fault it was?
Can you swallow your pride
    and be the first to speak?

Deliberately cut out anything
    that hinders purity or chastity
    at the heart of you.

And no profane expletives,
    but be as good as your word.

He seems to set impossible standards.

But he is more than teacher;

    he lived this deepest Law,
    he practised what he preached
    and was himself the Message.

'Repent and believe the good news', he said.

The good news is
    that he is more than Teacher,
    more than Message,
    he is Saviour.

And by his saving and forgiving grace
    you can make a new beginning,
    with his love working in your heart.

Mark actually wrote that Jesus was 'angry'; a later copyist changed the verb to 'had compassion on him'.

TOUCHING GRACE

When he saw the first patch
 he tried to ignore it;

  but soon he could no more avoid the numbing truth:
  he was victim of that disfiguring, dread disease.

His family were weeping as he left
 to live in a cave outside the village;

  and early every morning
  his mother or one of his sisters
  left a bundle of food at the agreed place,
  and turned away, weeping,
  while he watched from a distance.

At first they shouted any news;
 later they just waved or trudged away.

Some days he was not there,
 and they thought he had met others
 also ostracised, isolated, alone,
 condemned by fear
 to live on the edges of community.

Was Jesus angry with the leper for approaching him,
 or with the Law that forbade it?

Or was he angered by the leprosy
    that isolated his brother man from others?

Was he angry to be asked to heal
    (when that was not his primary mission),
    or because the man said 'If'?

'Of course I will' he said,
    and touched him.

It was so long since anyone had touched this man,
    so long denied the warmth of human contact.

This was no brief and timid finger-tip touching,
    afraid of any contagion;

    but a steady grasp upon his shoulder,
    a firm and gentle hand upon his head,
    only for seconds but it seemed like hours.

Years of isolation melted away;
    the separateness was bridged;
    and back in the world of living men
    he felt his leprous body whole.

How could he tell no one save the priest?
This man had given him life and hope again.

Jesus always welcomes your approaching him,
    always responds according to your need.

Have no doubt that he will help,
    and holds you with his sure, strong, steady love.

Luke's version of the Beatitudes is shorter than Matthew's and so is more likely to have been delivered on a single occasion. It is spoken on the level rather than a hillside.

PLAIN SPEAKING

He looked at his motley crowd of followers,
    so many poor or frail, exploited or abused,
    and hanging on his every word;

    his words were revolutionary,
    overturning accepted standards:

    being blessed is better than being happy.

Happiness can be so fleeting;
    things may so easily go wrong and spoil it.

This is not the best of all possible worlds for being happy
    but it's perfect for learning faith and love.

Poverty is no blessing
    – unless you choose it . . .

    but suppose you are spiritually bankrupt:
    to know you need God's help is a blessing.

You say 'Somebody should do something about it';
    but who should?
Seeing injustice and wanting it put right is not enough.

You won't be satisfied
    till you yourself are doing all you can
    for justice and peace.

Sorrow is no blessing,
    but it can be used for good;

    his 'mourners' have no self-pity,
    and help is promised
    to those who share others' grief and troubles.

If you take all this to heart
    you may well suffer for it;
    but you may well be nearer
    to being what you're meant to be:

    and that will be a blessing.

On the other hand,
    whatever you set your heart on
    you will probably get –

    verse 24 means paid in full already;

    and if, in the pursuit of happiness,
    what matters most to you
    is to be well-fed, well-clothed, well-housed,
    with 2.4 children,
    you may well achieve it –

    and nothing more.

PICTURES OF LOVE _____

If we take this literally
    Christians will be bruised and ragged and penniless!

(Many of his first followers were
    – overtaxed, dispossessed, exploited;

    they were not supposed to be:
    'God intends you to be clothed and fed and confident'.)*

These pictures are sermon illustrations,
    relevant to their time and traditions,
    and his meaning was very clear to them.

Matthew stresses the *right* cheek,
    and the only way that a right-handed person
    can hit you on the right cheek
    is with a back-handed blow
    – which is a double insult to a Jew:

'Even when people insult you to the uttermost . . .
    you must keep on loving them. . . .'

Dressing children for nativity plays
    needs several blankets and safety pins;

* See page 87.

that cloak was a desert nomad's birthright
— a defence against sand by day and cold by night
— it was written in their Law.*

'Even when they have taken every stitch which the Law allows,'
    said Jesus,
    'you must love them enough to give them more. . . .'

It was very much resented
    that a Roman official could compel anyone
    to accompany him for one mile for his safety's sake:

    'But,' said Jesus,
    'you must love him enough
    to go even further than he has any right to ask,
    and be glad to help.'

All this illustrates
    what 'loving your enemies' means.

It's the essential heart of Jesus' new teaching,

    and it's not easy.

It's hard

    to be kind and forgiving
    with people who have hurt you very deeply;

    to be patient and tolerant
    with people you don't like;

    to want only the best
    for people you're afraid of.

It's very hard but it's necessary.

In the Family of God, the children take after their Father!

* Exodus 22:26, 27

GOOD FRIENDS

Most weeks they would call to see him,
    singly or in pairs.

Outside the house and walking home,
    they talked of how he was,
    remembered earlier times they'd shared,
    expressed dismay at his paralysis,
    and wondered what had caused it.

At times with other friends of his
    they said how sorry they were
    and regretted nothing could be done.

Then they heard that man from Nazareth
    was returning to Capernaum:
    and thought that he might help.

They met and planned together
    and agreed a time to meet.

Their friend was not so very heavy
    but they'd not done this before –
    sharing the weight, keeping him level,
    matching their pace to each other.

They saw the crowd around the door
    but after all this hope and effort
    would not be put off.

A flake of plaster fluttered down but no-one noticed;
    then another, and another, and several more;
    Jesus stopped talking and they all looked at the roof.

A small hole appeared; then hands appeared, pulling at the
    mud
    and laths, making the hole larger and larger still; then all the
    light was blotted out until they saw a mattress being
        lowered!

Jesus saw the man on the bed and looked up,
    saw four eager faces watching through the hole,
    and because of *their* faith – healed the paralysed man.

The story highlights our common mission.

There are many whose lives are paralysed,
    whose only hope is if someone gives them a lift;
    sometimes they need several people working together.

Many in our neighbourhood
    need churches working together.

We need to share the load,
    and match our pace to each other.

And *we must not be put off*
    even if the way seems barred.

When Churches Together meet
    the ecumaniacs generally appear;
    but attendances and support are often small
    because other Christians are 'so busy'.

Our working together is vital;
    it concerns the priorities and the resources of the Kingdom.

The needs of the people,
    and the imperative of the Gospel,
    demand unity of us,
    and challenge our faith.

LET'S BE POSITIVE ⸻

Luke was not a Jew as Matthew was,
    did not understand about the *right* cheek
    or about the birthright cloak,*
    but he understood very well about loving.

'Love your enemies'
    is Jesus' brand-new teaching:
    – no-one had ever taught that before
    or seen how undiscriminating love must be.

Loving your enemies
    does not require desiring, admiring, or even liking them;
    but it does mean wanting for them
    the best that can possibly be.

If you pray for people who have hurt you,
    who have hurt you very deeply,
    and hold them before God
    in faith and love,
    in that positive, active, good will –
    you can't really hate them any more.

His ethics are so positive.

My childhood teachers insisted
    'Don't drink; don't gamble;

* See page 80

don't smoke; don't swear;
don't do this; don't do that.'

It was all so very negative
we called it the 'Do not spit department'.

But Jesus' golden rule is positive:
he is more concerned
with what he can add to your life,
than with prohibitions.

He calls us to go out of our way
to do positive good.

He wants us to be known by the good that we do
and *not* by the bad that we don't do.

But do not be surprised,
if 'when they see the good you do,
they' do *not* 'give glory to your Father in heaven'
– a thought of God may not cross their minds;

they may simply think you're kind or soft
or just take you for granted
– but so did their fathers to the saints.

Jesus' call to forgive your enemies
is about 'giving as good as you get'
not from what you get from them, but from *him*.

And you get as good as you give:

he will forgive you anything, everything,
for nothing is 'unforgivable'
– except to refuse to accept it.

It may be more blessed to give
    but it is much harder to receive
    – especially humbly to receive
    the forgiveness that you need.

In the light of his forgiving love
    you can forgive anyone.

DON'T WORRY

'You can't serve God and money'
    will come as a surprise
    after a generation of learning money matters most.

Countless catalogues on your doormat,
    tempting food adverts on TV,
    longing for a windfall or a lottery win,
    all suggest we've got the wrong perspective.

The institutional church has failed to meet the need;
    and searching people don't know where to look.

Some psychologists suggest
    our obsession with food and clothes
    implies a longing for security,
    because we're nervous about the future:

    but confidence does not depend on mammon.

He stooped down
    and picked a small purple flower,
    twisted the stalk slowly in his fingers,
    and gazed at it:

'Just look at that' he said,
    'the perfection of it,

the form and detail,
the colour and shades of it . . .

and there's a whole carpet of them,
the fields are covered . . .

and they'll be gone in a week!

They are not essential
but just for your delight
– and his.

Doesn't that tell you about him –
his love of beauty and colour and variety,
his benevolence and prodigality,
his delight in his creation,
his amazing fathering-forth care?
You can trust him.

God intends you to be fed and clothed and confident,

not overfed while others starve,
or overdressed with homeless on the street,
or fat-cats while there are so many poor,

but he knows what you need before you ask –
you can trust him.'

Don't worry about tomorrow
for you or for your children
for the church or for the world:
all our tomorrows are in God's hands.

'Don't worry about tomorrow'
does not mean

'Living as if there is no tomorrow'
for ourselves or for the planet.

But you've quite enough to cope with today:
each day has troubles enough of its own.

Each day has blessings enough too –
that's worth remembering.

Second Sunday before Lent
Ordinary 8

Year B: *John 1:10-18*
Alternative: *Mark 2:13-22*

Levi is Matthew. He did not himself write the Gospel that bears his name but collected and wrote down much of Jesus' teaching that forms so large a part of that book.

SINNERS' FRIEND

No God-fearing, self-respecting Jew
  would associate with Levi;

    ordinary people despised or hated him,
    some blamed him for their poverty;

    this tax-collector had some friends,
    but most were hoping for a 'favour'.

Jesus went to his house,
  knowing it would scandalise the scribes.

The ordinary 'people of the land',
    'sinners' because they did not keep the scribal laws,
    did not go to the synagogue,

    and so he went to them;

    many synagogues were being closed to Jesus,
    rejecting his message,
    and offended by his lifestyle,
    by his predisposition to the poor.

He was branded as outcast,
    sneeringly labelled 'sinners' friend':

but he cannot be judged by the company he keeps.

Not going where he was needed,
    he went where he was needed most.

Here is a man,
    loved by people of all ages,
    fun to be with,
    never pompous or ostentatious,

    and with the secret of being truly human
    which enables you to let the barriers down,
    and be yourself –

    even the barriers you are not aware of,
    realising a potential you never dreamed of,
    as Levi did.

This is the man for others,
    not to win support or to convert them,
    but just because he loves them.

Accepting them, though not their values,
    making allowances for human frailty,
    this is the transforming friendship
    that accepts, forgives, sets free.

This is unconditional caring – without strings,
    identified with us, and costly.

On a Friday afternoon,
    you will find him
    where he always is –
    amongst the outcasts,
    alongside the suffering,

    hanging on a cross,
    which is where you need him most.

This is one of the five 'Nature miracles' which are in a different class from Jesus' works of healing. They each have deeper meanings. There are always three questions to ask of narratives like these: what did it mean for those who were there? What did it mean for those who wrote it down, and what does it mean for me?

IN A STORM _____

He has never done that for me!

There have been few but some storms in my life;
    times when dark clouds have gathered,
    and my sky gone black;
    my little boat has seemed about to sink,
    and I've been very frightened.

I've cried for help:
    but he didn't seem to hear or care;

    and never once has he dispelled the storm
    with a commanding word;

    I've had to hang on
    by the skin of my faith's teeth
    till the storm has passed.

It seems to be a common experience:

God can seem very near,

but more often far away,
or even non-existent;

mostly God is 'hidden'
and sometimes very well hidden indeed.

Then I came to see
   that he was in my boat with me.

I have to look at what this story means
   in the light of my own experience,
   though trying to explain it
   must *never* mean explaining it away.

Gospel writers used it as proof of his divinity
   and that he is Lord of nature.

It doesn't prove anything for me
   though I'll keep an open mind.

I can never believe in magic,
   but I believe in miracles
   and miracles do not have to be spectacular.

Jesus asleep in the boat
   is a symbol of serenity and calm,
   not that he doesn't care.

Whether he calmed the winds or not,
   he calmed the disciples.

That's the miracle for me –
   that Christ with his peace
   was with them in the boat;

and he is in my little boat with me,
with me in the midst of the storms,
and he can give me peace.

We don't trust him enough.

WISE BUILDING _____

They hugged themselves with glee,
    some laughed out loud,
    as they imagined the man staggering about,
    with a plank in his eye.

They nodded wisely
    when he talked about the wisdom of the teacher;
    and muttered approval
    when he stressed that actions speak louder than words.

But he wanted more than acquiescence
    or to entertain;
    he wanted to be taken seriously.

Every preacher and teacher knows the feeling.

Sermons carefully prepared,
    phrases and timing well-rehearsed,
    and you preach your heart out:
    but comments overheard later in the porch
    suggest they haven't heard a word!

A teacher plans a lesson carefully,
    decides the aim and how to get there,
    prepares all the needed resources,
    and in the classroom goes through it step by step:
    next week they don't remember!

So much seems to fall on stony ground
　　or gets choked by many other things.

Knowing the risks,
　　the farmer kept on sowing
　　and so did Jesus.

Jesus knew his Palestine and its climate,
　　how an attractive site by the river
　　can become a raging torrent in winter;

　　and he had learned from Joseph
　　the importance of deep foundations.

I had to learn the hard way.

Experience has contradicted
　　some things I was taught as a child in church;

　　some things I was promised
　　proved to be no more than shifting sand.

Many of my generation are the same;
　　rejecting some of what we were given,
　　we hold to the rest more fiercely,
　　believing 'more and more about less and less'.

Christ alone
　　is the Rock on which I stand
　　and cling to in the storms.

And he still calls:

Why do you call me Lord and not do what I say?

Have you no faith even now?

Could you not keep awake for one hour?

You are my friends – if you do what I command you.

Sunday before Lent　　　　**Year A:** *Matthew 17:1-9*
Transfiguration Sunday　　**Year B:** *Mark 9:2-9*
　　　　　　　　　　　　　　Year C: *Luke 9:28-36*

Deep division between Jesus and the Twelve – they could
not accept his ideas about a Messiah who would suffer. After
six days of growing tension, there was only one thing to do –
take it all in prayer to Abba.

ON THE MOUNTAIN TOP ——————

Simon thought he must be dreaming:
　　but could see it all quite clearly;
　　and James and John were as unnerved as he –
　　it was awesome.

There was Jesus,
　　his Jesus,
　　all white and dazzling –

　　but there were two others there
　　in this ethereal light
　　whom he had never seen before:

　　could they be Moses and Elijah,
　　Moses from a thousand years ago,
　　Elijah from 800?

Whenever you come,
　　(with or without your friends)
　　to pray with him –
　　it is always so.

Christ brings you,
    beyond time and space,
    to the very edge of eternity,

    and Moses and Elijah are there,
    and all the great ones of old,
    and saints, and apostles, and martyrs,

    and all those you love but have not seen awhile . . .
    all who are 'beyond our horizons'
    – all are there:
    ten thousand times ten thousand.
It's breath-taking.

You come to pray with him,
    and in the mystery of his love
    he joins you with all the company of heaven.

On that mountain-top
    there is new light for Jesus,

    and for his friends –
    they see him in new light.
There's more to him than they had realised
    – he is more than Teacher, Rabbi, Leader, King. . . .

And when you come to pray with Christ
    there is new light for you.

Bring your problems, tensions, fears to Abba
    and you will see . . .
        Christ more clearly,
        new light on fears until they are dispelled,
        and a new perspective on your problems.

The more you see of Christ,
    the more loving you yourself will be,

    transfigured and transformed by love,
    till you become what you are meant to be.

And help is given:

Elijah thought he stood alone for Yahweh,
    and enemies sought his life;
    and Moses who demanded 'Let my people go'
    had offered his own life
    to save a disobedient people.

From all of history
    those two best understood what Jesus faced
    and could give help.

And those three disciples were given
    not what they wanted but what they needed.

In that unearthly mist, shot through with light,
    the shekinah-overshadowing of the Lord,
    a strong voice –
    'This is my Son. Do what he says!'

The promise stands
    you too will be given the help you need –

    not Moses or Elijah or an angel
    (unless you really need them!);

    perhaps not even a voice,
    ('voices' can be deceptive).

Sometimes there seems no answer
   and nothing more is given,
    because already you have all you need
    and he will not waste resources.

In answer to my pleading he has said:
'I've given you feet – get walking!
I've given you hands – you lift it!
I've given you a mind – you work it out!
I've already given you all you need.'

And he has said,
   in answer to my prayers:
'You feed them.
You forgive them.
You help them.'

So often
   the answer to our prayers
   is within ourselves, already given;

   but I promise you
   if you need more than you already have,
   help will be given
   for what you need
   – which is not always what you think.

LENT

Eternal God,

    in Christ you are beside us,
    sharing the pressures,
    understanding our needs,
    our fears, our restlessness,
    our hungering.

Some we have brought upon ourselves,
    some you have driven us into.

Make this quiet time and place
    an oasis for us,
    a time of renewal and refreshing,
    a time to put down burdens,
    and to find truer perspectives,

    a time to give our whole selves to you
    and to find strengthening.

'Forty days and forty nights' is a Hebrew figure of speech, implying a long but indefinite time.

A TRUE LENT

Keeping Lent is to 'imitate Christ',
    not slavishly mimicking him
    with forty days' privation,
    but doing what he did.

He needed time and space,
    to be alone,
    for prayer and fasting,
    for testing experience,
    and for choosing.

It was not exactly 40 days,
    marking them off with scratches on a rock,
    ('that's 28; only twelve to go!'),
    but he needed a long time.

For as long as he could remember
    he had an increasing awareness
    of a special work he had to do.

    but in this new experience of 'Abba'
    he needed time
    to wrestle with what it meant
    and decide what he must do.*

* See Lent 1, page 107.

Lent is to do what Jesus did:
    to examine what you are and do
    in the light of the Father's love.

The gospels point us inwards,
    to where the Kingdom,
    and your prayer room,
    and your real problems are,

    where wild beasts roam,
    – like envy or jealousy or malice –
    and where God is.

Though self-denial and self-discipline
    have their proper place,
    Lent is more positive than negative,
    more for 'taking on' than for 'giving up',
    making more time to pray –

    and if that involves denying something else – so be it!

In stillness of that solitary place,
    which can seem like a wilderness,
    look at yourself and all things
    in the light of the Father's love.

Lent is about potential,
    about what you can become,
    about what you have it in you to be and to do,
    restoring the lost image of God, with his help.

Imagine you could choose
    whom you would like to be or emulate: you can!

We have it in us to be like God;
    and because he is there within you
    strength is given.

Choose the way of love.

First Sunday of Lent

Year A: *Matthew 4:1-11*
Year B: *Mark 1:9-15*
Year C: *Luke 4:1-13*

How do we know what happened when he was there alone?

It was probably on the way to Jerusalem or in the latter days near Ephraim that his disciples asked him how it all began.

He told them of his wrestling in the wilderness. He used a classic three-part story form so that they might understand – and remember.

EXPECTATIONS

Being 'tempted as we are'
    means he understands our struggles
    but these temptations were especially *his*.

He needed time and space
    to decide what he must do.

For years he'd had a growing awareness
    that he could be Messiah;
    and he had learned that God is like a Father,
    but never with the depth and intensity
    of this experience of Abba.

In the wilderness
    he fused the two ideas;
    he wrestled with what was expected of Messiah
    in the new light of the Father's love.

In the desert beyond Jordan,
    where the flat white stones
    looked like cakes of bread:

    'Messiah when he comes
    will meet all physical need . . .'

    but if you live the way of love
    you cannot settle for instant material benefit,
    you have to care for wholeness,
    and you cannot bribe people.

In the hills where the plains of Esdraelon,
    scene of Israel's greatest victories,
    lay before him:

    'Messiah when he comes
    will lead a great army of men and angels
    and restore Israel's greatness . . .'

    but if you live the way of love
    you cannot bully people
    or force them to do what you want;
    he chose the way of non-violence.

In the distance, the sun glinted
    on the pinnacles of the Temple:
    'Messiah when he comes
    will have supernatural power . . .'

    but in the way of love
    you cannot brainwash people:
    they must be free to choose
    and will get no special treatment.

He chose the way of love,
    to be like Abba,
    but he knew his testing had only just begun.

He told his disciples about all this
    because there are parallels for his Church:

    Don't treat people as less than they are
    or try to force them to do what you want;
    don't ignore the bits of Scripture you don't like
    and don't expect any special treatment.

It means mission as well as ministry,
    outreach as well as fellowship,
    healing as well as teaching.

And don't compromise love
    for the sake of relevance or popularity.

He wrestled with people's expectations:
    but what do they expect of you?

So many pressures and problems are caused
    by what parents expect of their children,
    what children expect of their parents,
    what neighbours expect of you,
    what society expects of the church,
    or the church expects of its ministers;

    and what you expect of God,

    or what you think God expects of you,

    and most of all what you expect of yourself.

Don't settle for less than you can be;
    don't try to be what you can't be;
    and don't expect what is not promised.

God does not threaten you with a big stick,
    or want you to feel guilty,
    or ashamed or afraid.

All he expects of you
    is that you trust him . . .
    and do what he says.

A PRAYER IN THE WILDERNESS _____

Lord, have mercy on us.
Christ, have mercy on us.
Lord, have mercy on us.

Lord, have mercy on your Church and me.

Forgive our failures in love
    and for falling short of what we are called to be.

Forgive us
    for treating people as less than they deserve,
    for trying to make people do what we want,
    for asking what you have not promised.

Lord, hear our prayer

    for bread for the hungry,

    for peace among the kingdoms of the world,

    for the Church in the wilderness.

And in your mercy

    fill us with your love

    until there is no room in us
    for anything save love:

    no envy, resentment, or bitterness,
    no grudges or grievances,
    no fear,

    no room in us or amongst us
        for anything but love.

This is the third of four stories that John links together, and all are variations on the same theme. As usual in this Gospel there are many interwoven cross-references and much symbolism. But from this deep conversation the basic message is very clear.

IN THE DARK

He came at night
    and he was in the dark.

This wise old man,
    gracious and God-fearing,
    and looking for the restoration of Israel,
    respected member of the High Court,
    meticulously faithful to the Law,
    is in the dark.

Intrigued by Jesus,
    and quite friendly towards him,
    he wonders if this could be Messiah,
    and is ready to believe but can't commit himself:
    there's so much he doesn't understand.

And the answer is quite simple:
You need a new beginning.

The light that Jesus brings to dispel our darkness
    is a new quality of life,
    new ways of thinking,
    new ideas, new standards,
    creating a new community.

It's so completely new and different
 from what any pious Jew could understand,
 it can only be compared to a fresh birth
 – a new creation.

They talk of God who is Spirit,
 who is beyond our understanding,
 who cannot be constrained or confined,
 for as the wind blows where it will,
 so there are limits to how God works.

He comes to different people
 in different ways
 and none is more authentic than another.

None is superior to any other:
 there are no second-class citizens
 in the Kingdom of God.

Being 'born again'
 cannot be limited to one experience
 or to any one style of experience.

It means being open to his ideas,
 committed to his way,
 and trusting his love.

And everyone,
 even a faithful old man,
 needs this new commitment to him,
 this new birth,
 this new beginning,

 and everyone needs some help.

'Man's power is only man's power when all is said and done;
only God's power is strong enough to help a man to live in
God's Way.'   *Alan Dale,* New World, *page 361*

FOLLOWING CAN BE COSTLY _____

The days at Caesarea Philippi
    were a watershed in his ministry.

He now spent most time with the Twelve;

    after what happened in Galilee
    and his reappraisal of his mission,
    he had new things to share with them.

He led them deeper into his truth,
    taught them of Abba and how to pray,
    about humility and the ways of the Kingdom.

That autumn, he did not know in detail
    what would happen the following March
    but the risk was ominously clear.

Now he began to teach them
    that the way of Love could become the way of suffering,
    for loving always involves suffering,
    and it is costly.

It was hard to keep up with him
    as he strode towards Jerusalem,
    and harder still to keep up with his thinking.

'If you come with me
    you will have to be ready to die
    – for me and for the Kingdom.'

They had always known that they might be killed
when they fought with him against Rome;
but the emphasis now was different.

There and then it meant being ready to die;
    here and now it means 'dying to self';
    and it is still costly.

'Having a cross to bear'
    does not refer to a bit of rheumatism
    or an awkward relative
    but involves self-sacrifice.

It may well be that following him
    has proved more costly than you first thought,
    not only in time and money
    but in 'wear and tear'.

Sharing 'the fellowship of Christ's sufferings'
    may involve facing apathy or ridicule,
    being misrepresented or abused,
    and it hurts.

It may well be that following him
    has not worked out as you expected,
    and this surprising Christ
    has led you in unexpected ways.

He still has much to teach you
    of his mind and of his ways.

Alan Dale wrote this most perceptive paraphrase:

'If you want to help me,
    you must give all your heart to it.

You must put yourself last.
You must be ready to let people do their worst to you,
    and you must keep your eyes on me.'

Keep your eyes on him.

An unusual pairing of sayings of Jesus from very different times – the first towards the end of his Galilean ministry and the other near the end of his work in Jerusalem.

WARNINGS _____

All the Pharisees were not against him.

Some were so afraid of him
    that soon they were plotting to get rid of him
    with Herodians whom they hated
    – Loyalists and Republicans not simply negotiating
    but actually working together in common cause!

But there were different kinds of Pharisees
    and they were not all against him.

We should not generalise or label people.

If someone says 'I don't like Americans',
    or 'I don't trust Germans',
    or 'I can't stand the French',
    the answer has to be
    'Oh, have you met them all?'

Herod was very suspicious
when he heard what Jesus was doing:
'It's like John the Baptist all over again', he said.

Perhaps he sent the warnings
    but Jesus would not be intimidated;
    he still had much to do.

When 5000 met him by the lake,
    Jesus knew he would never lead that army
    nor ever be the kind of king they wanted,

    so he went away again.

He spent the next four months alone,
    and all that time
    was careful to avoid where Herod ruled.

He would not be intimidated
    but his time had not yet come,
    nor was this the place.

Jesus loved Jerusalem
    and especially its Temple,
    heart of the faith in which he grew.

He came at his Barmitzvah and for several festivals.

He ministered in Jerusalem
    from Tabernacles to the feast of Dedication,
    October to December in the year before he died.

He came deliberately on a donkey,
    still hoping people would turn to him.

Jesus wept for his Jerusalem,
    divided by self-righteous racial prejudice,
    putting its trust in military might,
    filling its coffers at the expense of the poor,
    because they did not recognise God's moment
    when it came.

He still weeps over our cities
    when we do the same.

In the last of his first quartet of interwoven stories, John's account of the well-side conversation is beautifully crafted and perceptive. There are also many deeper meanings.

AT JACOB'S WELL

Tired of others' abuse and condemnation,
     she used the farthest well
     in the hottest part of the day
     to be sure she was alone.

That day she almost panicked –
     someone was sitting by the well!
Then with relief she saw it was a man –
     he would not disturb her.

Quietly she approached,
     gently walked round behind him,
     and bent over the well;
     and then he spoke:

     'Can I have a drink of water, please?'

Surprised that he would dare to speak to her,
     and be prepared to share her cup,
     she was intrigued by his reply;

     she is, in turn, curious about his claims,
     insistent of her own beliefs,
     defensive to keep him at a distance;

and to evade the embarrassment of her life-style
begins religious argument.

He will not be diverted by theological debate,
      but because he wants to set her free
      he makes her face her self and who she is;

      and he makes her face his claim and who he is.

Slowly she discovers for herself,
      this is no ordinary Jew, nor Rabbi even,
      but a prophet, and even more than a prophet.

Believing him to be Messiah,
      she seeks the very folk she was avoiding:
      'Come and see for yourselves.'

His work is accomplished at Sychar.

John brilliantly interweaves his stories and themes:

'Water' links this well with the jars at Cana,
      with John the Baptist, and Jesus' disciples baptising
      and with the talk with Nicodemus;
      noon-time and Jesus' thirst deliberately link with Golgotha,
      the uncleanness of the woman's cup with purification jars,
      and true worship with the promised new Temple.

At the deeper level of religious dispute
      between Jews and Samaritans,
      the Incarnate I AM confronts them both,
      Samaritans now as previously the Jews.

He supersedes all that has gone before.
He is the end all longed for,
      and in him alone the place of true worship.

What he has to offer is without parallel:
    the well of living water to sustain
    the new life that he brings.

'Can I have a drink of water, please?'

In that simple request
    long-standing walls of prejudice were breached
    for he will tolerate no divisions
    of race or religion, of class or gender,
    or any irrelevant rivalries.

Your response to any plea for help
    may lead you to encounter Christ.

We may put up barriers
    – as she did – as we all do –
    to keep him at arm's length,

    but he will not be diverted
    for he wants to set you free.

Like her, you have no secrets from him
    for he knows all about you,
    – more than you have realised –
    and he wants to set you free.

He is not only asking for help
    but offering help and healing.

He wants to make himself known to you

    – so take the barriers down.

WORSHIP

Worship is a gasp of wonder
  or a cry for help.

Worship is saying 'Thank you'
  or 'Please'
  or saying 'Sorry'.
And meaning it.

Worship is responding,
  spontaneous or planned;
  your responding to Beauty,
  or to Goodness,
  to Suffering,
  or to Need,
  to Truth,
  or to Love.

Worship is in silence or in singing,
  in stillness or in dancing.
It is in laughing or in crying.
It is bowing down in Awe
  or Penitence
  or standing to give Glory.

It is the most important thing you ever do.

Worship is the opening of your inner self
  to God, who is beyond, beside, within you.

Worship is taking down the barriers,
  abandoned or afraid,
  and laying bare the heart of you
  to the burning and the healing,
  the breaking and transforming,

the mercy and serenity of God.

Worship is encounter with God
   in any of his thousand ways
   . . . and responding.

Unlike the other gospel-writers, John sets the 'cleansing of the Temple' at the beginning of Jesus' ministry rather than in the final days. The deeper meanings of the story best fit in that position with John's initial themes.

RE-CALLING _____

He came like an avenging angel,
    angry that the poor were being exploited,
    and even more that Israel denied its calling.

To buy a dove would cost a full day's wage
    but a 'guaranteed unblemished dove',
    alone acceptable for sacrifice,
    would cost three full weeks' wages –
    and could only be bought in the Court of the Gentiles:
    it was a racket!

Temple tax was two days' pay
    but Gentile coins bore 'graven images'
    and it cost another day's pay
    to have your money changed into Temple coinage.
It was blatant exploitation of pilgrims!

From all parts of the Roman world they came,
    Gentile proselytes, attracted to Jewish faith
    by Jews they met in their home towns;

    excited to come to their great Temple,
    they found the only place

they were allowed to go to pray
was like a noisy market.

That fired his anger most.

Neither Gentile coins nor Gentile people were welcome.
Called to be 'a light to the nations',
    the people of God were denying their mission.

The Lord had suddenly come to his Temple,
    as Malachi had promised.

He drove the sheep and cattle out:
    his new Temple has no need for animal sacrifice
    now the Lamb of God is offered.

'In three days' links with Cana,
    where imperfect religion is superseded;*
    and through his Resurrection
    he is himself the spiritual Temple
    where God is truly worshipped.

His friends recalled a Psalm about Messiah
    but the Sadducees were angered by his claim
    and used it in evidence at his trial.

'Destroy this Temple' he said – and they did;
    persisting in avarice and prejudice,
    they brought destruction on themselves.

If profit matters more than people
    and prejudice more than unity,
    these things lead to death.

* See page 52.

It's not about church bazaars
    or dual-purpose buildings
    or even Sunday selling;
    it's much more serious than that!

Still he challenges his Church:
    if we set profit above people,
    if we let prejudice hinder unity,
    if we neglect our mission,
    we shall bring judgement and destruction on ourselves.

The Lord whom we seek has come to his Temple.

THE PERSPECTIVE OF FAITH _____

'I haven't been to church since my son was killed.'

'How can anyone believe in a God
    when innocent people are butchered by tyrants
    or die in terrible accidents?'

'How can you say there is a God of love
    when he allows famine, earthquake, and flood,
    when good people die from incurable disease,
    when children are abused?'

If you asked a shepherd in Galilee
    the quickest way to Beer-sheba
    he'd probably say
    'I wouldn't start from here!'

Challenged with the problem of suffering,
    often arbitrary and quite undeserved,
    or the fact of so much injustice in the world,

    Jesus would probably say the same:

    'Don't start from there.

Begin with the revelation I have brought
    that God is your Father
    and you can trust him.'

The appalling things that can happen in our world
    remind us of our vulnerability, our frailty and mortality;

    for Jesus these uncertainties
    were yet another occasion
    to affirm to the only certainty he knew
    – to turn to Abba.

He had no simple answers;
    but he alone of all the great religious leaders
    would not avoid or evade the problem;

    he had his own way of dealing with suffering
    as Gethsemane makes plain.

Begin with Abba:

    your commitment to him
    may not solve the problem
    or answer the questions,
    but it gives you new perspectives and priorities.

He is the only unshakeable Rock
    on which to stand to face the storms of life,
    or to cling to in the darkness.

Turn to Abba

    and you will find no detached, unfeeling Deity,
    hurling misfortunes upon you,

    but a tender Father,
    on his knees beside you,
    sharing the grief,
    and helping you rebuild your life
    amid the ruins of earlier hopes.

Trust him.

This is regarded as one of the five 'Nature miracles' because a man who is born blind needs more than restoration.

A NEW CREATION

Disciples ask 'Who was to blame?'
　　and focus an age-long question;

　　but the compassion of Jesus
　　will not be diverted by theological debate.

People in need have first priority:
　　'This man should be able to see
　　– let's find out what difference God can make.'

　　he would never evade suffering for himself
　　but, faced with another's,
　　he always moved to practical action.

Too often we look for a 'fault',
　　for someone else to blame.

Too often still it seems
　　his disciples prefer talking to action,
　　conferences to compassion,
　　meetings more than meeting need.

Sound theology is very important

because what we really believe
shows in what we are and say and do;

and careful planning
is a vital part of Christian action,
as long as we talk no more than necessary
and do as much as possible.

The question remains
'Why do innocent people suffer?'

Those born severely disadvantaged,
    forced to 'trail a wing' through life,
    often give and evoke more joy and love than others:
    but that is no justification for their plight.

The wonders of genetic engineering
    may find the long-sought answer;
    science may soon identify the gene and intervene for health,
    but the engineers need watching.

Back in the healing story
    the leaders were hidebound by regulations.
Sabbath rules forbade handling clay, or healing the sick,
    and specifically 'spittle on eyelids'.

The Jews resorted to abuse and threats to get their way;
    but the man-made-whole saw them quite clearly,
    and his protest is a warning:
    'You don't listen when people talk to you, do you?'

In John's hidden meanings
    the water of Siloam develops his interwoven theme;
    and the clay deliberately mixed with spittle
    recalls the 'dust' of Genesis creation:
    this is a new creation.

A man born blind cannot have sight *restored*:
    in a notable 'first' Jesus *gives* him sight,

    and not only sight but wholeness –
    for when he answers 'I am'
    he echoes the incarnate Word,
    at one with Christ – and like him.

These are the marks of the new creation.

THE OFFER OF LOVE _____

John makes a parable of the brazen serpent,
    forged by Moses at God's command,
    and raised amongst a people plagued by deadly snakes.*

It was not a forbidden graven image,
    nor an idol to be worshipped,
    but a sign of the deliverance,
    which God offered to a penitent people.

So also in Christ,
    crucified and so exalted,
    God offers to the penitent,
    not only the sign, but the reality
    of healing and deliverance and life.

Quite often in a televised crowd,
    John 3:16 is placarded.

Presumably, the bearer hopes
    that someone will recognise the reference,
    know where to look it up, read it,
    and respond.

It may not be your chosen way of witness
    but many regard this one sentence
    as the best and simplest summary of the Gospel.

* Numbers 21:4-9.

God is Love beyond all telling,
    deeper and broader and higher than any can imagine,
    active Love that embraces all the world,
    all its people, all his creatures.

He gives all that he has
    so that they may share his eternal life.

In John's theology
    judgement is not reserved for the last day
    but takes place every day, here and now.

It is not meted out by a stern forbidding Judge,
    but of our own choosing;
    we bring judgement on ourselves.

It is not your heavenly Father's will
    that any one of his little ones should perish.

God condemns none to perish
    though we may condemn ourselves.

Adam, embarrassed and ashamed, hid in the bushes,
    just as none of us wants to be exposed;
    we prefer the anonymity and supposed security of darkness.

This age-long battle in every human heart
    comes to its climax at Calvary,
    when the cosmic conflict of darkness and light
    is resolved in the 'lifting up' of Jesus;
    and the darkness does not put out the light.

In the wilderness of a dying world
God offers deliverance and healing and life.

He does not punish unbelief.
Any condemnation is not his.
God offers life and love
for us to accept or reject.

The choice is ours.

No parable contains the whole Gospel but only one facet of it. In this story there is no costly Atonement and no Holy Spirit; but the nature of the Father is clearly portrayed.

THE PRODIGAL FATHER _____

This is the most misnamed parable.
It's not about either boy
    but about the father.

Here is a farmer
    who has two sons.

Like so many brothers they are chalk and cheese:

    one is adventurous, daring, careless, wasteful,
    and gets himself in a mess;

    and the other pedestrian and careful,
    prudent, unimaginative, perhaps rather boring,
    who stays at home and does his duty;

    but one has to wonder
    if he had any friends;
    and would he know how to make merry?

Two boys, chalk and cheese,
    and their father loves them both.

The younger one leaves home
   and has a wild time;
   sows his wild oats
   finds himself penniless,
   – and friendless;

   he comes to his senses,
   and goes back home;
   and his father goes out to meet him.

The other doesn't understand his younger brother;
   his angry outburst in the orchard
   reveals deep-seated jealousy and long resentment.

He won't share the family celebration,
   gets in a huff, and stays outside;
   so his father goes out to reason with him.

   That's the point of the story:
     the father loves both his sons
     and goes out to meet them both:

The older boy is very angry with his father,
   makes unfounded accusations and distorts the facts,
   – as we all do when we are angry or jealous –
   and he finally disowns his brother.

The parable is open-ended:
   there is no indication how he will respond.

Everything is grounded in the Father,
   who comes to meet us in our various needs.

He knows our needs before we ask,
   he challenges and confronts our sin and brokenness;

he calls us into a restored relationship
with him and with our brothers.

He welcomes and forgives;
    he challenges and invites.

He wants his family complete.

Fifth Sunday of Lent　　　　　　**Year A:** *John 11:1-45*
Passion Sunday

Near the climax of the 'Book of Signs' (chapters 2 to 12), the fifth of the magnificent seven 'I Ams' affirms that the new life which Christ gives is victorious over death.

BLESSED BY GOD _____

Martha speaks her mind,
　　and, feeling neglected, bluntly reproaches Jesus.

A prayer of protest is quite proper.

The prayer of Jesus at the grave
　　begins with thanksgiving
　　as all prayer should;
　　we take too much for granted.

But if, like the Psalmists or Job,
　　you have a complaint about arbitrary injustice
　　or the unfairness of it all,
　　it is right to tell him so.

Prayer is a dialogue of learning;
　　in the stillness you learn more
　　about yourself, and God,
　　and the way things really are.

You may come to understand
　　'Why should it happen to me?'
　　is answered 'Why should it not?'

　　and 'Why me?' becomes 'Why not me?'

'Jesus wept' is not an oath;
    it expresses his grief at the death of his friend;
    for John it stresses the reality of the Incarnation.

This man is truly flesh and blood,
    who understands a cry of pain and anguish,
    and shares the pain and hurt of bereavement;

    if ever you are almost overwhelmed by grief,
    he understands and shares;
    and comes to you as he came to Martha and Mary.

The long story about Lazarus
    whose name so aptly means 'blessed by God'
    is the crowning sign of victory over death.

A nobleman's servant is dying,
    the man at Siloam is as good as dead,
    and Jesus speaks the word of life.

Here Lazarus is dead and buried and decaying,
    and this resuscitated corpse is a further sign:
    Jesus not only speaks of the word of life
    but himself is Resurrection.

Often a solemn voice reminds us
    that in the midst of life we are in death;
    but Jesus' commanding voice insists:
    In the midst of death we are in life.

Don't worry about what happens when you die
    for he is Resurrection.

And there is more to come.

Offering you a chalice, a minister may say:
    'The blood of Christ keep you in eternal life.'
    – keep you where you already are.

That's John's new theology and understanding
    after sixty years of prayer and meditation.

Eternal life is here and now;
    we have passed from death to life already.

One may feel half-dead
    through bereavement or despair,
    divorce, disappointment, or redundancy,

    and find a new lease of life
    that seems like resurrection,
    life that is fuller and richer,
    more satisfying and fulfilling,
    eternal in quality as well as quantity,
    here and now.

God is in the business of raising the dead,
    as Easter will make plain.

Life is a succession of deaths and resurrections;
    and when you come to the end of your days,
    and he holds you through death into Life,
    it will be but one more
    in a whole series of resurrections.

He calls your name,
    and wants you free;

    he is loving you to life.

In the other gospels the account of the cleansing of the Temple follows that of Jesus' triumphal entry into Jerusalem. John has already used that story (2:13-22) but this encounter with Greek pilgrims make the same point.

The second part of this lection is John's parallel to the 'agony in Gethsemane' in the synoptic gospels.

TRUE GLORY

Greek readers would be pleased
    to see their fellow-countrymen part of the story.

Surprisingly Philip was not sure how Jesus would respond.

His best friend, Andrew,
    himself invited to 'Come and see',
    had a growing reputation for bringing others to Jesus
    and was quite sure.

He remembered other Gentiles: a Roman centurion,
    a Syro-Phoenician woman, a Samaritan leper, and others;
    he remembered Jesus in the Temple
    insisting that Israel must be a light for all the nations.
'Of course he will', he said.

Seeing is more than meeting;
    seeing is understanding;
    and seeing is believing.

By the metaphor of the dying grain of wheat
   Jesus made plain that only after his death
   will all people see him clearly;

   and, please God, come to believe.

The dying grain refers not only to Jesus,
   but to the calling Israel had betrayed,
   and what he expects of his disciples.

'My servant shall be where I am'
   is not only a promise of eventual paradise
   but a call to the way of the cross,
   to sacrificial service here and now.

The crisis had now come.

He was in turmoil
   at the awful prospect of what he had to face
   to draw all people to himself.

An immediate voice from heaven,
   as at his Baptism and Transfiguration,
   strengthened him to endure the cross;

   and confirmed to all who can hear
   that divine glory is revealed
   in his ministry and in his death.

John's profound perception
> sees that being crucified is being glorified.

Glory is not in splendour or power,
> such as Daniel dreamed of and the Jews expected,
> in the irresistible conquest of the Son of Man.

Think not of radiance or effulgence,
> or a shining brightness beyond description.

We see the glory of God in the face of Jesus Christ,
> not as on Damascus Road or Transfiguration mountain,
> but in the sweat and tears and blood of Gethsemane,
> and the torture of the cross.

This is as much as you will see of true glory,
> till you are in a greater light and on another shore.

Fifth Sunday of Lent   **Year C:** *John 12:1-8*
Passion Sunday

John weaves together the different stories from Mark and Luke. He sets his version of the story prior to the 'Triumphal Entry into Jerusalem', so that, taken together, they are a 'sign' of death-and-resurrection.

ANOINTED KING _____

While his friends chatted over supper,
    Jesus was so preoccupied with other thoughts,
    he seemed a thousand miles away.
Mary felt the dark clouds gathering.

From sitting at his feet,
    hanging on his every word,
    she had come to know him so well.

She knew why he had come to Bethany:
    he would go into Jerusalem for Passover
    and into danger;

    and if his enemies came
    he would not fight or resist them.

She had bought some very costly spikenard,
    the lingering perfume of a king,
    mixed it with a little olive oil,
    and sealed it in an alabaster jar
    for just such a time as this.

She poured perfume over his head;
    some dripped on to his clothes,
    some on his feet;
    she loosened her headband
    and wiped his feet with her hair.

The reaction of the others was appalling.

Always keen to earn some favour,
    they were clearly jealous.
They envied Mary's generosity
    and wished they'd thought of doing it!

The gibe about the poor
    was made in jealous pique
    and Jesus' rebuke was justified:
    they seldom showed so much concern about the poor.

John can be most vindictive;
    he is as ruthless with Judas as with the Jews:
    Judas became a scapegoat for their common failure,
    but snide remarks about him thieving
    were nasty and unnecessary.

Why do we add insult to injury
    when we find someone to blame?

Why do we get jealous so easily
    of someone else's perception
    or sensitivity
    or generosity?

When at last we look into his eyes
    his first question will be about the poor
    who are still with us:

the key phrase is noted by Mark:*
'whenever you want to'!

O, to be like Mary
  taking his words to heart,
  sensitive to what he is doing,
  and pouring out for him
  the very best we have.

* Mark 14:7

Sixth Sunday of Lent
Palm Sunday

Year A: *Matthew 21:1-11*
Year B: *Mark 11:1-11*
Year C: *Luke 19:28-40*

In 164 BC a victorious Judas Maccabaeus rode into Jerusalem, purged the Temple of heathen desecrations, and established their religious freedom. The rededication is still celebrated in the Jewish festival of Chanukkah.

THE SHEPHERD KING

Jesus came riding to make Jerusalem choose.

It was deliberately planned and staged
    recalling Maccabaean liberation
    and Zechariah's prophecy;

       and 'cleansing the Temple'
       on the following day
       underlined the parallel.

The people went wild
    and sang the song their fathers sang
    to welcome Maccabaeus.

But they didn't see the donkey!

The Romans saw the donkey
    and were glad it was a peaceful demonstration
    – the city was packed and highly charged,
    like a tinder-box awaiting a spark.

The Zealots saw the donkey
    and were bitterly disappointed
    – they hoped he would ride a war-like horse
    and not a docile donkey.

But the people saw only a victory parade,
    riding as Zechariah promised,
    and welcomed him like a king.

Why do we only see what we want to see?
Why do we only hear what we want to hear?

When Jesus comes riding
    he claims to be King,
    for only a king may ride into the city
    – all others must dismount in deference.

This is the King of Glory,
    but not such glory
    as Rome, Jerusalem, or we ourselves would think:

    no pomp or splendour,
    no finery or trappings of majesty,
    no 'sapphire throne'.

True glory is
    in service with a towel and a basin,
    in obedience in the garden,
    in self-sacrifice on the cross.

This unexpected and surprising King
    turns our ideas and values upside down.

He comes on a donkey,
> with the secret of peace –
> peace on earth,
> peace in society and in church,
> peace of mind,
> and peace with God.

The secret of his peace
> is not a sword but a cross.

Not peace at any price,
> for some things he must stand against
> and others he must stand for:

> against any prejudice of race or class,
> of religion or of gender,
> against possessiveness,
> against profiteering or power-seeking;

> and *for* the way of love,
> of service and of sacrifice,
> of loving enemies and forgiving hurt,
> the way of non-violence,
> that makes true reconciliation.

This is the King of Love.

A LITANY FOR PALM SUNDAY

The congregation is asked to hold their palm cross in the right hand, STAND, and hold the crosses high.

Minister   Hosanna!
All   Hosanna in the highest!
  Blessed is he who comes in the name of the Lord.

Minister   Lord Jesus Christ,
  we raise these palms to greet your coming,
  these crosses to adore your love.

Minister   Shepherd-King of Peace
All   we greet your coming with joy.

Minister   Eternal King of Kings
All   may your Kingdom come.

Minister   Royal King of Love
All   come and rule in our lives.

Minister   We believe
All   in the sign of your Cross you will conquer.

Minister   Gladly we affirm
All   Jesus Christ is Lord.

Minister   Hosanna!
All   Blessed is he who comes in the name of the Lord!

Suggested hymn:
  Lift high the cross, the love of Christ proclaim

FOR CHILDREN IN HOLY WEEK _____

So much happened between Palm Sunday and Easter Day that children who are in church on those two Sunday mornings will find it hard to know the what and why and how of it all.

Adults may follow his journey step by step, until they see in the goodness of Friday the truth that sets people free.

But not the children.

The following may be used in a responsive dialogue on Palm Sunday or in a take-home paper to help them grasp something of those seven days that changed the world.

On Sunday the Shepherd-King came riding,
    on Monday, he cleared the Temple court,
    on Tuesday, he was teaching his disciples,
    on Wednesday, anointed King with oil that Mary brought.

On Thursday, he had supper with his friends,
    he washed their feet and gave them bread and wine;
    that night he was betrayed, arrested, tried,
    abused and scorned – and still showed Love divine.

On Friday morning, he was crucified
    forgiving those who nailed him to the 'tree',
    all-loving till the moment that he died,
    undying love to set the whole world free.

He died as he had lived,
    the perfect way of Love,
    still faithful to the Father's will,
    victorious love to prove.

NEXT SUNDAY IS EASTER AND HE IS BACK WITH HIS FRIENDS

THE PASSION OF OUR LORD _____

Jesus did not have to die.
It was not all planned and predetermined.

Everybody had a choice
   – and everybody chose:

    Judas, a well-meaning but mistaken friend,
    Caiaphas, a devout and sincere man of God,
    Pilate, a ruthless and unimaginative politician,
    superficial crowds, baying for Barabbas,
    . . . everybody chose,

    including Jesus.

If it had to be,
    he would choose the time and place:
    it must be in Jerusalem and at Passover.

And he chose to be obedient
    to the Father's way of love.

He faced the supreme uncertainty of death
with faith but with no knowledge of what is beyond.

And he set way-marks for us
through the common human experiences
of being deeply hurt,
or desperately wanting to know what to do next,
or struggling with grief,
or an unacceptable situation beyond our control,
or deep dissatisfaction,
or running out of vitality,
or being afraid of death . . .

and his way of love
leads to wholeness and hope,
belonging and confidence,
vitality and victory and peace.

Jesus did not come to die;
he came to love.

Through all the growing hostility and hatred
this is the truth he will not disown.

Deny and desert him,
deride him, denounce him,
he will not stop loving.

Kill him,
and to his last gasp
he will not stop loving.

Golgotha is the awful fruit of human wickedness;

    it placards up for all to see
    the effects of violence and force,
    self-preservation, compromise, and betrayal.

Standing before the Cross
    I slowly come to see
    that sins like mine
    are cluttered at its foot.

It is as if I had denied and betrayed him,
    scourged and mocked him,
    shouted 'Crucify',
    hammered home the nails.

And I kneel.

That Friday afternoon
    he was where you will always find him
    alongside the outcasts,
    with the suffering and the dying;

    and even in this extremity
    he was ready to offer them
    compassion, and comfort, and hope.

He himself was almost overwhelmed by suffering

    and so he can share all our pain,
    understand all our hurt,
    is alongside us in any need.

In reality the isolation and the darkness
    was far worse than any earlier speculation.

With Mark and Matthew,
  I recoil from the sharp cost of the Atonement
  and that desperate cry of dereliction,
  God god-forsaken.

With John, I stand in awe
  before the mystery of a cosmic battle,
  while the whole creation holds its breath
  till the precarious outcome is resolved,
  and he flings that great triumphant shout
  against the darkened sky:
  'It is accomplished!'

Most readily I kneel with Luke
  before the Saviour of the world,
  needing so much to hear his whispered words
  of forgiveness, and hope, and peace.

In Christ crucified,
  crucified by us and alongside us,
  I find the deepest truths revealed.

Here is man as he is meant to be,
  completely obedient to the Father,
  faithful and loving to the end.

Here God reveals himself as he really is,
  his very Essence and Nature:

    no stern Judge demanding a death penalty,
    nor self-centred Absolute,
    no unfeeling Principle,
    nor a distant Monarch,
    but an aching Father.

God is eternal Love,
    precarious and vulnerable,

    with such serenity
    as can accept, absorb and transmute suffering
    and make it a means to heal and bless,
    to deliver and redeem.

Here, for me,
    all theories of Atonement fall away,
    or else all come together,
    I 'see the Lamb in his own light'
    and realise though I know not how
    that he was crucified for me.

This is the Saviour of the world,

    who forgives anything, everything,

    who gives hope for the next step and beyond,
    in the confidence that all is in the Father's hands.

A DIALOGUE OF THE SEVEN WORDS

These verses are suitable for a public dialogue of eight voices as well as for private meditation.

They have been used on several occasions following a 'tenebrae' extinguishing of seven candles, each reader in turn responding to one of the 'Words' and relighting one of the candles following their spoken response.

Leader: The seven last Words of our Saviour from the cross;
each gives new light to those in darkness.

Voice 1:   **Father, forgive them;
they do not know what they are doing.**

Voice 2:   This is what I need to hear:
forgiveness for my wrong.

Sometimes I know quite well what I am doing.

Deliberate disobedience or ignorant hurting:
I need to know I am forgiven.

Voice 1:   **Truly I tell you:
Today you will be with me in paradise.**

Voice 3:   This I need to know –
Christ with me facing death;
companionship and confidence
when all seems lost.

Him at my side along life's way:
Christ with me
and me with Christ
today.

Voice 1: **Mother, there is your son.**
Friend, there is your mother.

Voice 4: This is what I need to hear:

the caring that will make me strong;
Love telling me that I belong
among his friends, his family,
to care, support, encourage me.

Voice 1: **My God, my God,**
why have you forsaken me?

Voice 5: Though there are times when God seems near;
when life is black and hope seems gone
then where is God?
He's so well hidden, he seems not there at all.

I need to know
this loneliness is nothing new.
Such desperate isolation comes to most,
and in the darkness all there is to do
is cling to Love,
and trust him still.

Voice 1: **I thirst.**

Voice 6: I hardly know what hunger is;
But there are many things I want,
things even that I need;

I also need remember
that often others care;

and always there is one
who shares my need.

Voice 1:   **Father,**
into your hands I commit my spirit.

Voice 7:   I need this word of confidence,
this peace in face of dying,
this trusting as a little child.

In anything that life may bring
or death,
I need this faith:
that all is in the Father's hands
and nothing can part me from his love.

Voice 1:   **It is accomplished.**

Leader: This is the word all need to hear
though death has done its worst
and Christ seems broken.

Love has met sin,
and sin has been forgiven;

Good has met evil,
and evil has been mastered;

Life has met death,
and death has met its end.

The atonement is made,
the reconciliation is accomplished,
the victory is won,
the truth made plain,

and the times have turned.

EASTER

Light has met darkness
    and the darkness has not put it out.

Love has met sin
    and sin has been forgiven.

Life has met death
    and death has met its end.

Alleluia!

An additional prayer for Sundays in the Easter Season is printed on page 209

EASTER DAY

All years: *John 20:1-18*
or A: *Matthew 28:1-10*
B: *Mark 16:1-8*
C: *Luke 24:1-12*

EASTER

Easter is the vital heart of Christian faith.

Some find the miracle of Resurrection beyond belief,
but the evidence is overwhelming,

far more than for the effectiveness of seat-belts,
or the dangers of smoking cigarettes.

There is healthy disagreement in the narratives,
but Easter faith does not depend
on the claims of his friends
for the stories themselves are statements of faith.

Nor does Easter faith depend
on the fact that so many people believe it,
or on the validity of a cloth in Turin,
or even on whether the tomb was empty.

The real evidence
is the New Testament itself
for without a Resurrection not one word would be written;

the Church that wrote it still exists,
and is itself essential evidence –
no human institution could survive so long;

and so many lives have been changed encountering Christ.

Easter faith insists
    that though Caiaphas is dead,
    and Pilate is dead,
    and Judas is dead,
    and the Temple long destroyed,
    and the Roman empire fallen,
    Jesus is alive;

    not a fading memory of his disciples,
    or them carrying on where he left off,
    but that Christ himself is very much alive.

Easter does not put right
    what went wrong on Friday,

    for by raising him to life
    God confirms Good Friday:

Good Friday was right,
    Jesus was right,
    the way of love is right;
    the way of the Cross is vindicated.

By the Resurrection,
    God says 'Yes' to Jesus;
    to all he said and did,
    to the promises he made.

By the Resurrection,
    God says 'Yes' to you in him,
    affirms that you are forgiven,
    and confirms the hope and help,
    the victory, and peace, and confidence
    which Jesus promised.

Mary could not have moved the stone,
　　but wanted just to be alone with him,
　　in her private grieving.

Like so many since,
　　she did not expect to meet him,
　　and so she did not recognise him,

　　until he called her name.

Peter and John in the tomb
　　remind me of Plato's cave,
　　with but the shadows of reality:

　　there they are, uncertain what it means,
　　in the place of fear and darkness,
　　of isolation and sadness;

　　those things are all there, in the tomb,
　　but Christ is not:
　　he is up and out and gone,
　　alive in the light of a bright new day.

A church can be like them,
　　pottering about in half-light,
　　amid the things of what is past and gone,
　　looking for him in the wrong places,
　　while he's abroad in the world,
　　calling us into the light of his new day.

It was all so unexpected and breathtaking
　　they needed weeks to begin to understand;
　　and we shall need these Easter weeks at least
　　to explore what Resurrection means.

Jesus did not conquer death:
    he was dead,
    really dead,
    and God raised him to new life.

This is an entirely new thing which God has done;
    the beginning of a new creation.

It is not limited to Jesus,
    or what happens when you die;
    just as 'we make his Love too narrow'
    we limit Resurrection too.

More than his promise of life beyond death;
    he offers life of eternal quality
    here and now.

This is what God is doing all the time.

He is loving people to life,
    not only at the end of days but every day;

    and when he holds you through death to life
    it will be but one more
    in a whole series of resurrections.

Easter means
    he offers you a new beginning,
    a new world for you
    and a new you for the world,
    new peace, new light, and new perspectives,
    a new lease of life
    today.

The last word is not with death but with Jesus.

THE LORD IS RISEN! _____

Fleeing from the garden,
    most struggled back to Bethany;
    Peter and John hid in Jerusalem.

Now Sabbath and the Passover were over
    it seemed safe to mingle with the others in the streets;

    slowly, and separately, they came to Mary's house,
    still afraid they too might be arrested
    and suffer the same fate as their Master.

Still in grief and shock,
    they shared the horror of what had happened on Friday,
    and planned their return to Galilee.

Then Jesus came.

Those significant scars convinced them
    and they welcomed him with shamefaced joy.

He breathed Peace over them:
    a peace dispelling doubt and fear,
    of knowing their betrayals were forgiven;
    peace binding them together and to him,
    nerving them for coming days.

When they found Thomas
    they told him excitedly, repeatedly;

How he wished it was true

but he had to know for himself:
Easter faith is personal.

Thank God for Thomas
with his enquiring mind and probing finger.

Capable of great devotion,
he is still called 'doubting Thomas'
as if doubt was a discredit.

But doubt is not improper,
doubt is normal;

uncertainty is natural;
searching questions are right;
those who admit no doubt are far more worrying.

Thomas came to faith,
but not to proof,
for there is no proof or guarantee.

Confronted by the risen Christ,
his insistent demands faded away;
he didn't need to poke his finger
for he knew.

Thomas came to faith
only because he stayed with the other disciples,
with those whose experience he wanted to share.

In times when doubts assail you,
or your faith burns low:
for God's sake, don't leave the church.

Stay with the company of Christ's friends:
nowhere else are people saying,
'The Lord is risen!'

Hold on by their faith
till it is your own.

EMMAUS ROAD

So often things don't work out
   as you expected, or hoped, or planned;

   then Christ comes alongside you,
   sometimes uninvited,
   often unrecognised,
   and opens up a new and unexpected future.

He alone is not overtaken by circumstance
   and can work all things together for good.

Aunt Mary and Uncle Cleopas
   were trudging home,
   mostly in silence, despondent and dejected.

Their dismay and disappointment
   was political as well as private:

   so much hope for their nation,
   its freedom and its future,
   were focused in their favourite nephew.

Now it had come to nothing;
   hope was gone, the dream was shattered.

They had known him since he was knee-high,
    but in the half-light they did not realise who he was.

He brought them a brighter hope
    and a wider vision.

He brought new light on Scripture,
    a new way of looking, a new understanding;
    he made it come alive.

'You have Moses and the prophets',
    all you need if you know how to look;
    but we look for wrong things in the wrong places.

You will only make sense of the Bible
    if you read it in the light of Christ.

They lit the lamps;
    when he took the bread and said the blessing
    they saw the nail-marks in his hands!

And then he was gone
    and left them wondering.

It is so often this way:
    you sense his presence but for a moment –
    was it illusion or reality?

They rushed back to the disciples
    to share and test their experience,

    and found their hopes confirmed
    in the fellowship of his friends.

Luke gave his story priority
   for those who had never seen Jesus:

Invite him to your heart and home
   and he will come.

Hold to the Church, to Word and Sacrament.

He will break new light on Scripture
   and come to you in the breaking of bread.

THOSE GLORIOUS SCARS _____

His coming is almost 'played down':
    they are talking quietly, incredulously, together,
    and then they realise he is there.

There is an amazing restraint
    about the Resurrection;
    no blast of trumpets
    heralds the new creation.

This is the way God usually works –
    quietly, unobtrusively,
    almost unnoticed, often unrecognised,
    and with great humility.

What sort of body is this?

He cannot be touched by Mary 'until he is ascended'.
    but invites the touch of Thomas,
    and those he met in this room;

    he is no ghost but 'flesh and blood'
    and can eat fish;

    he can pass through walls and locked doors
    (so had no need to move that Stone
    except to show that he was gone);

    and he can appear and disappear at will.

Seen only by those who love him,
    is it only because he is unexpected
    that he is so hard to recognise?

What kind of body is this?

Easter faith asserts that Jesus lives
    but claims nothing specific about a resuscitated corpse
    or defines what a 'resurrection body' is.

How can we understand life in another dimension
    or this glimpse of a new creation?

We are facing mystery.

When he held the bread at Emmaus,
    and in the upper room,
    and especially with Thomas,
    the marks in his hands and feet,
    wounded for our transgressions,
    bruised for our iniquities,
    are the signs by which he is recognised.

We need to explore more fully
    how the presence of the living Christ
    is best identified by the marks of suffering Love.

A living Church,
    alive to Christ, alive in Christ,
    will show the same marks of Love.

'Bearing in our body
    the dying of the Lord Jesus'
    means living the way that Jesus died.

Jesus comes as morning breaks; that is typical for John for the risen Christ brings new light and a new day.

IN MORNING LIGHT _____

On the Lake:

Simon, like most people after bereavement,
    felt they should be getting back to work.

It was a long, frustrating night.
Perhaps they had lost the knack;
    but they'd known trips like this before.

As morning broke,
    a man was walking by the water's edge
    and called to them;
    it was not unusual.

Nor was it unusual
    that he could see, as they could not,
    the early sun glinting on the fins of fish;
    that was not unknown on Galilee either.

They had never seen so many fish.
It was taking all their strength to hold the net
    and haul the catch the man had pointed out.

John was not working with the other six,
    but just standing in the bow of the boat, staring;

it all seemed so familiar, like déjà vu;
and then the penny dropped.

He reached behind him to grab at Simon,
who couldn't wait to row ashore,
but was so eager to get to the Master's feet
– until he saw the charcoal fire
and all the guilt of his denials came flooding back.

Eager to please,
though he felt nothing could atone for his denials,
he dashed to fetch some fish as Jesus asked,
and landed the whole catch with his own strength.

But he said little during breakfast.

Deeper meanings are quite clear:

Christ comes to us when we are at work,
with the light of his new day,
though we may need to be still and looking hard
to recognise his coming.

When we are frustrated or just tired,
or feel we have achieved so very little,
he comes, often in familiar things.

From his perspective on our situation
he can see things that we can't see;
and often what we are looking for,
or the answer to our problems,
is under our very noses.

It will take all our strength,
working together,
to do what he points out to us.

But whatever we do
we cannot make up for the mistakes we've made.

After breakfast:

I love chocolate cake.
I love my wife.
I love my minister, David,
    and I love the Yorkshire Dales.

But these are different kinds of loving
    my wife would not want to be classed with cake,
    nor my minister with a dry stone wall.

These are different kinds of loving
    for which English language has but one verb,
    while the Greeks had four!

After breakfast,
    Jesus strolled with Simon,
    who was kicking at the stones,
    his head bowed.
And the conversation went like this:

'Simon Johnson,
    do you love me more than the others do?'

(Simon was more humbled now)
    'Lord, you know I am your friend.'

'Then feed my lambs.'

A second time: 'Simon Johnson, do you love me?'

'Lord, you know I am your friend.'

'Then tend my sheep.'

And a third time: 'Simon Johnson, are you my friend?'

Peter was hurt that at the third asking Jesus said,
    'Are you my friend?':
'Lord, you know everything. You know I am your friend.'

    and the conversation continued as John records.

He uses your own real name, and no nickname,
    in your encounter with him;
    for this is very personal,
    and very serious.

If you deny him,
    he will come seeking you,
    to meet your deepest need
    (which may well be to know you are forgiven).

He will commission you again to be his friend,
    until you can accept he is forgiving you,
    until you can accept and forgive yourself.

It is just between you and him;
    and if, like Simon, you start to feel uncomfortable
    and try to talk to someone else,
    he will not be diverted.

Don't compare yourself with others.
He calls you to be yourself,
    imitating no one else but him.

This is about you and your discipleship,
    about you following him.

He may well remind you:
'You are my friend, if you do what I command you.'

He is simply asking,

'_____ , *(insert your own name)*
will you do what I say?

It's that personal,
and very much for real.

THE GOOD SHEPHERD

All sheep look alike to me,
    but not to a shepherd.

The Good Shepherd knows your name
    and knows your need,
    does not confuse you with any other,
    and loves you –
    enough to lay down his life for you.

In a high-walled sheep-pen on the hills
    a shepherd sleeps in the narrow gap
    to defend his flock from danger;

    so Christ,
    who in Gethsemane pleaded, 'Let these others go',
    puts himself between you and danger,
    to save you from what preys upon you
    and from what could do you harm.

He will *not* keep you safe from every ill,
    his people may suffer disease like any other,

    but he will deliver you from fear and despair,
    from all he battled with in that Garden,
    from doubt and disillusion, sin and death;

he will keep you from being unforgiving,
from any resentment or bitterness,
and the things that could really destroy.

He expects us to follow when he calls.

So easily side-tracked by what looks inviting,
we get ourselves caught in some thorny problems,
entangled in guilts and fears,
but whatever the thicket,
he will come to the rescue.

He expects us to follow when he calls.

We would love to stay where we are,
in the warmth and security of the fold,
but he wants a pilgrim flock.

Like an eastern dragoman,*
he guarantees resting and feeding places
all along the way
if only we will use them!

The metaphor changes:
the Shepherd becomes the Lamb that was slain,
and the sheep are called to be shepherds:

'You must do as I have done for you':

seek the lost,
defend those in danger,
feed the hungry with the bread of life.

* See page 201.

Keep following him
    until in time, and beyond time,
    not only separated Christians
    but all of other faiths and none,
    are brought into the unity of one flock.

The Good Shepherd is leading us all
    to a better pasture than we have known.

THE TRUE AND LIVING WAY ─────────

How much we have learned
    since we began life's journey.

Some things we were taught as children
    we have proved true again and again;
    but some we can no longer believe.

I find I now believe
    'more and more about less and less',
    rejecting things experience has denied,
    but holding to some more tenaciously than ever.

Pause for a while
    and recall as best you can
    the truth Jesus has taught you,
    and the way he has brought you,
    and the life he has given you so far.

And give thanks.

When Jesus said
    'No one comes to the Father but by me'
    did he mean that only Christians would be saved
    or that non-Christians must all be converted?

We used to think
    that all of other faiths must turn to him;
    but now we have met some of them

and they have no intention of converting.
Does that mean there is no place for them?

Now we have met some,
    and admire and respect their faithfulness;
    there is much that they could teach us.

Christians could benefit
    from a similar obedience to that of Jews,
    a disciplined prayer-life like Muslims,
    from Hindu spirituality and Sikh acceptance,
    and Buddhish ways of meditation.

If Jesus did not exclude them,
    and they are among his 'other sheep',
    what did he mean?

Try to describe God,
    the Intelligence that conceived, imagined, and created
    every single thing;
    a deep, mysterious Being, quite beyond us,
    and soon we are struggling for words.

Jesus cut through this complex knot
    with one simple word:
    Abba.

The God who created everything,
    in whom we live and move and have our being,
    is as a Father to us;
    you can trust him as a little child.

Jesus alone taught this unique relationship;
    only he said God is Abba.

There are many ways of describing,
    and as many ways of approaching
    this God of a hundred names;

but if you want to call him and know him as Abba,
it can only be through Jesus.

Looking back is one thing;
    looking forward is very different.

The way ahead is not always clear.

Following the way of Jesus
    can seem like trudging through a desert;
    green fields and blues skies
    can turn into an arid wilderness,
    and familiar landmarks disappear.

All you can do
    is take the next step with Christ,
    trusting as a little child,
    trusting Abba.

Beware of those who think that they possess the truth
    or think that they are always right.

The truth about God is beyond us;
    he cannot be grasped, encoded, or encreeded;

    the whole of truth is more than we can grasp
    but we must keep on quarrying;
    the heart of truth is Abba.

All our life is in his hands,
    here and beyond our present horizons.

Trust him.

This is the last of the great 'I AM' sayings which John records. They are of such importance to him because they affirm and illustrate his central theme that Jesus is God, at one with the Father.

'I am the true Vine' is the profoundest of all seven.

THE TRUE VINE _____

They were so proud of the great golden Vine,
　　the symbol of God's chosen people,
　　emblazoned on the door of the Holy Place in the Temple;

　　but they made the sign invalid
　　and were denounced by prophets as degenerate;
　　because they did not produce the fruit
　　which God expected of his people.

Jesus makes the same protest
　　by the six imperfect jars at Cana,*
　　in his parable of the vineyard,
　　and by his cleansing of the Temple.

His new Israel must do better.

The vine which must be fruitful
　　is a symbol of the Church's mission.

Abundant, bright green leaves are not enough;
　　the wood itself is useless, fit only for burning;

* See page 51.

a church exists by fruiting
as 'a fire exists by burning'.

If there is no mission it is not a church.

Converts and growing congregations are exciting
and evangelism is incumbent on us all.

In days when membership declines,
a repeated trough in the Church's history,
there may well be growth in other ways and places;

but in times of falling congregations
it is also important to recall
numbers are not the only measure of fruitfulness.

More than six hundred disciples
left Jesus in a single day;
but twelve stayed for his 'words of eternal life',
and he himself stayed faithful.

Fruitfulness is not always measured in numbers
but in faithfulness.

His 'words abiding in us'
means we share his words and deeds,
his action and passion,
his death and resurrection.

To 'share the fellowship of his sufferings'
does not require we should be martyred;
it means living the way that Jesus died;

the pattern is set on Calvary –

to forgive even those who hurt us deeply,
to range ourselves alongside outcasts and the dying,
to build a caring fellowship,
to hold on in the darkness,
to share all human privation,
to keep loving till our last breath,
and to trust all things to the Father.

Christ is not the trunk of the vine,
    with us branching out from him;
    he is the whole bush,
    and his disciples part of him.

We can never say
    'The life went out of such-and-such a church
    when poor old so-and-so died!';
    for Christ is the life of the Church,
    forever flowing through it.

His people are part of him,
    in union with him,
    and have no life apart from him.

We preserve our union with him,
    and 'keep in contact'
    by private prayer and corporate worship.

'In the name of Jesus'
    is not a magic formula
    that guarantees a favourable response
    which we can 'tack on' to the end of any personal plea.

The prayer that is surely granted
    is prayer 'in his words',

prayer 'in his name' and character,
praying as he would pray,
praying with the mind and heart of Christ.

In worship
John is deeply sacramentalist.

His account of actions in the Upper Room
includes no institution of the Eucharist;
but he preserves, set by the Galilean lakeside,
a long exposition about the Bread of Life;*

and the first sign John records
is of the wine at Cana,
and this parable of the Vine
is delivered in the Upper Room.

Christ who is the life of the Church
nourishes his people through bread and wine.

When you come to the Lord's table,
it may look and taste like bread or wafer,
it may look and taste like wine,

you may feel that nothing has 'happened',
for there is no magic here.

But as, in faith,
bread and wine are shared
as Christ has commanded

he gives himself to you,
he lives in you,
he lives through you,

and he nerves you to be faithful
and bear fruit.

* John 6.

THE NEW COMMAND

He waited until Judas had gone,
   gone to betray his Master
   and his brothers.

Such betrayal was the very opposite of his new command.
He had to wait until Judas had gone.

He knew some sense of relief.

After all the waiting and wondering,
   after the testing and the turmoil,
   he would soon hand himself over
   and put himself at the disposal of his enemies.
The time for his glorifying had come.

John's understanding is unique:
   crucifixion and glorifying are one.

Since Easter we have come to see
   that this special Sunday did not put right
   what had gone wrong that Friday;
   because Friday did not go wrong.

He was glorified in his passion,
   as was the Father.

From childhood they had been taught
    to love God and love their neighbour;
    he gave this *new* command
    so they could support each other in such loving
    and for the sake of their fellowship and their mission.

He requires of them and us
    that we give freely to each other
    such love as he has given to us.

Just as he had washed their feet;
    and was laying down his life for them,

    he commands us to be ready to do anything for each other,
    service to the point of sacrifice.

This lection is set four weeks after his lifting up,
    where we can see most clearly how he loves,
    the love that will go to any lengths.

We see him forgiving the deepest hurt,
    bringing hope to those suffering and dying,
    creating new caring, new relationships.

He holds to Love in the deepest darkness
    and in the worst privation;
    and keeps on loving us until his final breath.

Loving as he has loved us,
    means living the way that Jesus died.*

* See pages 186, 187.

By his new command
    he binds us together
    so that our mission may be more effective.

Then and now and all through history,
    his Church has grown and grows primarily
    by the quality of his people's fellowship and caring.

'See how these Christians love one another'
    must never be said in derision
    but in wonder.

Love one another.

HELP IS AT HAND

Six months before he had warned them,
    but they would not accept it.

By the feast of the Dedication,
    they knew there was a risk,
    but didn't take it seriously.

Despite three months' waiting in the wilderness,
    and his sombre mood at Bethany,
    they did not think it would happen.

So, in the upper room,
    when he spoke clearly of his approaching death,
    they were bewildered, stunned and shocked.

Why do we not take his warnings seriously?
Why do we call him Lord and not do what he says?
Why do we not take his promises to heart?

He had to prepare them for what was coming,
    to try to dispel their fears,
    to give them new hope and lasting peace.

He spoke of his departure and return as one event.

They would soon see him again
    because they loved him.
(Only those who loved him saw the risen Christ.)

By his return and resurrection
   they would find new life,
   become spiritually alive.

He promised them the Paraclete.

Only in John's gospel is the Spirit called the Paraclete.

A paraclete is variously
   an advocate to plead the cause of the guilty,
   a counsellor to give advice and guidance,
   a comforter
   to give strength and fortitude,
   and always a helper.

The Spirit will do all of this and more.

He will help them to remember
   words that Jesus spoke,
   acts of love that Jesus did,
   that may have slipped their minds
   yet are the substance of the Gospel they must preach.

He will help them to understand
   more and more of the Truth,
   and Christ is the Truth that they must teach.

He will live and work within them,
   and help them become what they were called to be.

Unseen by the world,
   which cannot see Christ as he really is;
   unknown by any,
   except those open to his presence;

   he is the great Enabler.

Wherever you go, he is there;
    all the time of your life, he is with you and within you;
    pleading, guiding, helping,
    liberating, strengthening, enabling.

Don't worry;
    and don't be frightened.

NO GREATER LOVE _____

'You can be my friend – if you do what I tell you.'

No other friendship would survive for long
　　on such a basis;
　　but this is like no other friendship.

He shared his deepest thoughts with them,
　　taught them the best he knew,
　　confided his hopes and fears in them,
　　treated them as equals though they were not.

He had always loved them,
　　and now would show the full extent of his love,*
　　washing their feet,
　　laying down his life.

They would be friends of his
　　if they kept his commands;

　　but if they failed,
　　he would still be friend to them;
　　for he is friend of sinners.

The same is true for you as his disciple –
　　the same command and the same assurance.
He is the best friend you have.

* John 13:1 (NEB)

Our instinct for self-preservation is so strong
it is cause for wonder and great admiration
that anyone should willingly give their life.

Many are praised for laying down their lives
when in fact they did not die willingly.
Killed in war, their lives were taken from them,
sacrificed by a political leader or misguided general.

They did not deliberately sacrifice themselves
but there are many others who have done.

In every generation there have been some
who have chosen death before apostasy
and given their lives for their beliefs,
like twelve of the many martyrs of our own time,
so recently commemorated in statues,
on the front of Westminster Abbey.

Thousands of others
have humbly and willingly given everything
to save another's life.

On Good Friday, 1945,
Elizabeth Pilenko, that wonderful Russian nun,
took the place of a hysterical girl in the line
and walked into the gas-chambers at Ravensbrueck.

On holiday in 1968
Roger went to help his daughter,
who was struggling in the sea;
she was saved and he was not.

So many, known and unknown, remembered and forgotten,
in a moment of crisis have deliberately given themselves.

And what of those who give their lives
  in selfless, sacrificial care
  of an aged parent, a disadvantaged child or friend?

Thank God for all of these.

There is no greater love.

He who laid down his life for us
  calls us to the way of love,
  whatever it may cost.

GOING TO THE FATHER _____

We are coming to the end of these wonderful Easter days;
they can't go on for ever
but we need to take to heart what we have learned.*

'Going to the Father'
    is the crowning of Easter,
    and a sign of his continuing presence.

We have learned through Jesus
    that the unseen Father is close at hand,
    so involved with us that he suffers alongside us,
    but with a serenity that cannot be overwhelmed.

We no longer see Jesus
    but he has not gone away;
    he has come near,
    closer than breathing,
    nearer than hands or feet.

Christ is with you,
    on good days as well as bad;
    in your joys as well as in your sorrows,
    in leisure times as well as working days,
    when you are refreshed as well as tired,
    when you are still as well as in your travelling.

* See page 208.

'Going to the Father'
   is a sign of life beyond death.

Children, asking for a loved relative who has died;
   are sometimes told, 'He's gone to be with Jesus'
   hoping they ask no more!

There will probably be more questions
   but we have no more answers.

We do not know
   what heaven will be like;
   all the pictures are only guesses,
   including pearly gates and golden mansions.

Eventually, you will find Heaven is far better
   than anything you have dreamed of,
   and you will gasp with wonder.

All one can say of your departed relatives
   is that they are with Christ,
   and Christ is with you,
   and in Christ you are one.

'Going to the Father'
   means we are on the way
   to the final Resurrection of all things,
   when Christ will bring all things to unity.

We cannot understand that either,
   but we hold the faith
   that he will keep on loving
   until all things come to fullness of Life.

'Going to the Father'
     means Abba is at Jesus' end,
     as well as his beginning;
     and that all things are in the Father's hands.

Whatever dread or danger
     anyone brought to him,
     the response would always be the same:
     a gentle smile and the confident assurance
     'You are in the Father's hands.'

Mary wanted to cling to her risen Lord,
     as many won't let go of those they love.

We too would like to cling
     to the security of Easter days,
     but it is for our good that he goes;
     we have new truths to learn,
     and still greater things to do,
     beyond what we can imagine now.

When he goes to the Father
     he leaves us with but one tangible sign: broken bread;
     and with one word: Abba.

Who needs more?

J.C. RULES OK _____

If Christ is not ascended and glorified,
    the Incarnation loses its point,
    Atonement and Resurrection are of little worth,
    and faith and hope are vain.

Ascensiontide is as important as Christmas or Easter;
    its concept holds some very special meanings
    at the heart of faith and symbolised nowhere else.

This picture of a three-tier universe
    is in the language of poetry, symbol, and mystery;
    this ascending does not mean going up,
    save in authority and status.

A rich man, going on a far journey,
    would send a servant one day ahead,
    a sort of first-century Thomas Cook,
    to book resting and refreshing places
    for his master when he came – one day later.
That servant was called a dragoman.

The ascended Jesus is our Pioneer and dragoman,
    gone before to prepare a place for us;
    (if Christ is not glorified, nothing is prepared!)

The ascended Jesus is still Jesus,
    glorified but still Jesus;

there is now a man in heaven,
and he is still himself.

It means that beyond death I shall still be myself,
    not absorbed in some lump of spirit,
    but a perfected self, still recognisable,
    and those I know and love,
    who are beyond my present horizons,
    are still themselves, perfected,
    and I shall see and know them.

The ascended Christ, 'at God's right hand,
    ever lives and prays for us'.

That means, as prayer must always mean,
    he holds us in his love,
    wills for us the best that can be,
    and is always active on our behalf.

Ascension celebrates that Christ is King.

If the law and the environment allowed,
    I could well paint upon a wall
    'J.C. rules OK'

The last word is with Love,
    and Love is in control.

All things are held in Love,
    and he will bring all people and all things
    into a unity.

It seems almost impossible,
    a far cry from what now is;

but Ascension faith affirms it will be so,
for Jesus is not only living but Lord.

Ascensiontide proclaims
    he is gone to the Father,
    closer than breathing,
    nearer than hands or feet.

And you will never be alone again.

The last time they saw him,
    his hands were raised in blessing:

    and that's the way it always is –
    Christ always blessing his Church,
    and always blessing you.

Ascension alone affirms

    that he is always blessing us,
    working for us,
    holding us in Love,

    and will hold us through death,
    into life eternal,
    where we shall be perfected,
    with all we know and love,
    and with ten thousand times ten thousand more.

Ascension means supreme authority is his,
    all things in his control;
    Love has and is the final word.

It means he has gone before us,
    blazing a trail for us to follow,
    with refreshing all the way.

If we affirm that Jesus Christ is Lord,
    we must let him rule our lives,
    every part of us under his control;
    and we must follow where he leads.

Seventh Sunday of Easter **Year A:** *John 17:1-11*
Year B: *John 17: 6-19*
Year C: *John 17:20-26*

This is the only recorded long prayer of Jesus. Some have
suggested that it was composed either by John to draw these
discourses together or by a later teacher for Eucharistic use.
It is very different from the Gethsemane prayer recorded in
the other gospels but it is not improbable that Jesus prayed
in the upper room as well as in the garden. The themes are
unity and glory.

THE PRAYER OF JESUS _____

Five separate times that evening he had promised
    that they would be given whatever they asked
    if they prayed as he would pray.*

Before he went from the security of this room,
    out into the darkness, to suffering and death,
    the incarnate Son was communing with his Father

    and we may glimpse with wonder
    the beauty and serenity and intimacy
    of that relationship.

Only the essential unity
    and the shared glory of the father and the Son
    give real meaning to the cross
    and confidence of victory.

* See pages 187, 188.

He prayed for his closest friends,
    never doubting they would carry on.
He had taught them all he knew;
    the mustard seed was sown, the leaven was working.

They must be separate from the world,
    and exposed to the same dangers as he was:
    the servant is not greater than his Lord.

He prayed for them the resources
    which they needed to fulfil their mission:
    unity and glory such as he shared with the Father,
    the unity which is neither exclusive nor competitive,
    the glory made plain in compassion and love.

Even facing the horror and suffering
    which the next few hours would bring
    he could still speak of his joy,
    that deep serenity which none could take away.

He prayed the same joy for them
    in all the tribulations they would face,
    the joy of knowing his truth
    and proclaiming it in a hostile world.

The only ground of lasting joy
    is in such unity and glory as he shared with the Father.

He prayed the same for his future church
    of which we are a part.

He prayed joy for us
    in the glory of obedient service,
    even though we suffer for it.

And he prayed that all his Christians might be one,
    in a unity of love which transcends all differences,
    which demonstrates his reconciling power
    and proves the Gospel works.

When will *that* prayer be answered?

A SUMMARY OF EASTER MEANINGS ___

The living Christ comes
    to those closest to him,
    in any place, at any time,
    until they understand
    he comes in every place and all the time.

Whether they are alone or together,
    at home or at work,
    he comes,
    calling them by their own name.

He comes,
    unexpected and often unrecognised,
    unobtrusively and often unnoticed,
    to meet their deepest need.

He comes
    to the grieving with joy,
    to the fearful with peace,
    to those tired or frustrated with new perspectives,
    to those spent or disillusioned with new direction.

He brings forgiveness for sin,
    trust for doubt,
    hope for despair,
    and liberation from guilt.

He brings the new light of his new day
    on the Bible,
    on our personal situation,
    and on the fact of death.

He makes himself known in the breaking of bread;
    he invites us to share the fellowship of his sufferings,
    to use all our energies as he directs,
    and to live in the way that he died.

A PRAYER FOR SUNDAYS IN EASTER ___

Jesus of the garden, Living Lord,
    come to us;
    call us by our name
    and give us joy.

Jesus of the upper room, Living Lord,
    come to us;
    dispel our fears,
    breathe your Spirit into us,
    and give us peace.

Jesus of Emmaus Road, Living Lord,
    come alongside us;
    show us new truth,
    give us new hope,
    and make yourself known to us.

Jesus at the lakeside, Living Lord,
    come to us;
    help us to see what you can see,
    give us your perspective,
    and help us work at your directing.

Jesus of the mountainside, Living Lord,
    come to us;
    and as your blessing rests on us,
    help us to follow where you lead.

PENTECOST TO TRINITY —

Heavenly Father,
    fulfil our Saviour's promise
    and give us your Spirit,
    in wind and fire
    or as a gentle breath
    whichever best suits your purpose.

Ascended Lord,
    give to your church
    the variety of gifts we need
    to equip us for obedient service
    and to build up the body of your people
    until we may achieve mature unity.

Holy Spirit of God,
    within us and around us,
    nourish and grow in us
    the fruits of your indwelling
    until we ourselves are become like Jesus.

Pentecost

All years: *Acts 2:1-21*
Year A: *John 20:19-23 (or 7:37-39)*
Year B: *John 15:26-27, 16:4b-15*
Year C: *John 14:8-17*

BIRTHDAY

A celebration for the giving of the Law
  was added to the spring wheat harvest festival,
  for man cannot live on bread alone;

  we also need more than rules to live by,
  so the Pentecost outpouring of the Spirit was well timed.

The Spirit of God was there at the beginning,
  brooding over the face of the waters,
  bringing order out of chaos;

  he is always at work in his creation;
  and clearly rested on some special souls
  like Abram, Moses, Elijah, Jeremiah and Second Isaiah.
He is most clearly and fully seen in Jesus.

What happened at Pentecost
  was that ordinary mortals
  like Andrew, Simon, Philip, James,
  or like you and me,
  were enabled to become like Jesus.

Trying to describe what happened
    Luke used many intense symbols:
    noise and wind and fire and dove
    all represent the presence of God;
    tongues of fire are for a message to deliver;
    they rest on each because all share in the mission;

    many lands are represented there,
    in this antidote to Babel,
    because the message is for all the world;
    always some are contemptuous of God's messengers,
    even though they speak a universal language,
    which is the language of love.

This was an entirely new thing
    with a string of new consequences:
    a new community with new concerns and concepts,
    new characters and new compassion and new confidence,
    and new ways of communication.

It was the birthday of the Church.

Birthday of the Church it may be,
    but many Christians are shy of Pentecost.

Childhood talk of a Holy *Ghost* made them uneasy;
    the disciples seem to have lost control of all inhibitions,
    and we are wary of that;
    and most of all, this is a new thing
    and we don't like change.

The Pentecost experience is so hot and strong
    and we prefer it soft and gentle:
    but that's on offer too.

John later set the record straight:
    Christ breathing his Spirit on his disciples
    as in the upper room on Easter night.

Like a driving wind
   or a gentle breath,
   there is no limit to how he comes.

Nor are there any limits to the way he works.

Some in our time may imply
   that if your experience of God
   is not the same as theirs,
   you are not saved;
   without the gift of tongues,
   you are not Christ's;
   or they arrogantly claim their brand of faith is best.

It may be best for them,
   but there are no second-class citizens in the Kingdom of
      God,
   and no limits to the way he works.

Nor is he limited to the followers of Jesus;
   who else inspired Moses and Gotama,
   Mohammed, Confucius, Nanak?

There are no limits to the Spirit of God
   in time or place or people or experience.

The most famous detail of Michelangelo's painting
   on the ceiling of the Sistine chapel
   is the spark of life between the finger of God
   and the finger of man.
That's what happened at Pentecost.

If you dare to trust him enough,
   are not afraid of what he might do to you,
   and dare to reach out towards him
   as he reaches towards you,
   the sparks can fly.

You test the validity of his indwelling,
    not by feelings but by how loving you are,
    by how much you are like Jesus.

Jesus was the one really Spirit-filled man,
    and those who are born of the Spirit
    grow to be like him.

You have no idea
    how loving and patient and kind you could be,
    how really good and generous, reliable and reconciling,
    how gentle and gracious you can become,
    when the Spirit is working in your life.

You can be like him.

They needed time;
    until they were not surprised by his presence,
    or afraid of his guiding,
    or troubled by his demands;

    but sure of his presence,
    and longing for his Kingdom.

When, like Simon, you know you are accepted,
    and really believe you are forgiven,
    you are free to let your responding love
    reach out to meet his incoming love;

    and they will fuse together,
    and you will be transformed by Love.

Trinity Sunday

THE BEST IDEA YET _____

They had always known there is only one God.

After the Resurrection and the Pentecost experience,
    they were aware of God working in them
    and they had a different attitude to Jesus.

To affirm that Jesus is Lord
    is to say he is divine;
    and they'd got problems!

To say the Spirit was in them created problems
    but they could not deny their own experience.

It seemed like three Gods but there is only one.

The seeds of the idea are in the New Testament
    but they never mastered it.

Christians wrestled with the problem
    for more than four hundred years,
    argued about it in the taverns,
    even came to blows in Synod.

At last they found a formula;
    it expresses the idea of Trinity;
    but it doesn't explain it.

Their formula of three Persons in one Substance
 is out of date now anyway;
 we talk in terms of energy, not substance.

You can never understand it,
 but within this very complex idea
 is the most precious insight Christians have.

The experience that God is Abba,
 and that God is in Christ,
 and that God is within each of us,
 is very important.

The idea that God is Father, Son and Spirit
 is the most profound we have been given.

God is beyond, beside, within us,
 Source and Goal and Guide,
 creating, redeeming, enabling:
 this is so very precious.

The Trinity is Mystery,
 and we need this reminder that God is beyond us,
 always more than we can grasp.

We rejoice that Jesus is the Friend of sinners
 but we must not get too pally;

 variety in worship is important,
 but we must not get so clap-happy
 that we lose the mystery.

God is beyond us;
 we need to recover humility before him,
 we need to recover awe and wonder in our worship.

God is best described as Father, Son and Spirit
> but we must never forget that God is One.

There is Unity in the Trinity
> and he bringing all things into one.

The imperative of the Trinity
> is that we work
> for all that heals and unites,
> and against all that divides or destroys.

Just as God is One,
> we owe it to our mission
> that his people are one.

The idea of the Trinity
> preserves the breathtaking idea
> that the secret of all things is Loving;
> the heart of creation is active Love.

Before the world began,
> not an eternal committee for goodness' sake,
> but a Community of active Loving;
> each of the Three loving the other Two.

I can't understand that either
> but I know what it means.

The idea of the Trinity calls us
> to work at loving in all our relationships,
> always to ask what is the loving thing to do and do it,
> to work to build a community of love.

GOSPEL INDEX